Learning from Conflict

A Handbook for Trainers and Group Leaders

Lois Borland Hart, Ed.D.
LEADERSHIP DYNAMICS

Learning from Conflict

A Handbook for Trainers and Group Leaders

Addison-Wesley PUBLISHING COMPANY

READING, MASSACHUSETTS • MENLO PARK, CALIFORNIA
LONDON • AMSTERDAM • DON MILLS, ONTARIO • SYDNEY

Library of Congress Cataloging in Publication Data

Hart, Lois Borland.
 Learning from conflict.

 1. Conflict (Psychology)—Study and teaching.
2. Social conflict—Study and teaching. 3. Psychology, Industrial—Study and teaching. I. Title.
BF503.H37   158′.2   80-17227
ISBN 0-201-03144-2

ISBN 0-201-03144-2
ABCDEFGHIJ-AL-89876543210

To Arn:
whose example and support made this project possible

Contents

Planning for Conflict   201

Foreword

Fighting, hostility, and controversy, all of which can be called conflict, are nearly everyday fare for individuals and groups, although they do not always openly evidence themselves. Too often, there is emotional effort and involvement by many people that go largely unrewarded because they move in restrictive rather than constructive channels. By the same token, conflict releases energy at every level of human affairs—energy that can produce positive, constructive results. Two things should be recognized here. First, conflict is an absolutely predictable social phenomenon. Second, conflict should not be repressed, but channeled to useful purposes. Both of these realities lie at the heart of this book.

The goal of organizational leadership is not to eliminate conflict, but to use it—to turn the released energy to good advantage. The role of the trainer, human resource developer, and OD specialist is to help others analyze developments, and learn about why people behave as they do in conflict situations. This book gives resources, methods, and designs to make that role effective.

Conflict is almost always caused by unlike points of view. Because we have not learned exactly alike, and because we therefore see and value things differently, we vary in our beliefs as to what things are or should be. Because conflict, large or small, is inevitable, the extreme result at either end is a situation that is undesirably abrasive or dialogue that is creatively productive.

In 1976, the American Management Association* sponsored a survey of managerial interests in the area of conflict and conflict management. The respondents in the survey were participants in programs sponsored by AMA. The respondents included 116 chief executive officers, 76 vice-presidents, and 66 middle managers. The results of the survey strongly suggest that the respondents see conflict as a topic of growing importance.

- They spend about 24 percent of their time dealing with conflict.
- Their conflict-management ability has become more important over the past ten years.
- They rate conflict management as a topic of equal or slightly higher importance than planning, communication, motivation, and decision making.
- Their interests in the sources of conflict emphasize psychological factors, such as misunderstanding, communication failure, personality clashes, and value differences.
- They feel the conflict level in their organization is about right—not "too low" or "too high."

These executives and managers also revealed what they considered to be the principal causes of conflict within organizations.

- Misunderstanding (communication failure)
- Personality clashes
- Value and goal differences
- Substandard performance
- Differences over method
- Responsibility issues
- Lack of cooperation
- Authority issues
- Frustration and irritability
- Competition for limited resources
- Noncompliance with rules and policies

*Kenneth W. Thomas and Warren H. Schmidt, "A Survey of Management Interests With Respect to Conflict," *Academy of Management Journal* 19 (June 1976): 315-318.

Nevertheless, the reality that corporate executives and managers devote 24 percent of their working time to conflict management is considered to be quite low by school and hospital administrators, mayors, and city managers. In these and similar fields, conflict resolution commands nearly 49 percent of the attention of such officials. The causes of conflict usually are the same as those previously cited, but in a different order of rank. I also find that most leaders look upon conflict as a negative experience. This is the key to the problem. We should take pains to see that conflict is a creative and positive occurrence.

The author of this book points out the ways in which conflict can be a constructive process. The goal is to provide valuable learning experiences for all of us on ways to creatively manage and cope with conflict.

The concepts, steps, exercises, and designs in this book can be used in a variety of settings. Both staff and line professionals can apply these resources.

Conflict is a topic of increasing importance in all human systems. There are multiple reasons for this increasing importance, including: the growing scarcity of natural resources; the complexity and increasing interdependence of relationships between individuals, groups, organizations, and nations; the values and life style pluralism that characterizes people of all ages, sexes, and races; and the rising expectations and psychology of entitlement that are reflected in the motivation of employees, managers, owners, customers, and all others who interact in and with an organization.

The goal is to realize the importance of effective conflict resolution so that social change, growth, and consensus may continue to occur within the complexity of today's living.

Gordon L. Lippitt
Professor, School of Government
and Business Administration,
George Washington University,
Board Chairman, Organization
Renewal, Inc.

Preface

Conflicts are a natural part of life—without them, life can be boring; with too many, life can be stressful. The more we learn about conflict, the greater the chance of learning from them, reducing unnecessary ones, and managing future ones with more ease.

I didn't learn about conflict in any pat, efficient, or complete way. It started by watching my parents, brother, school friends, and teachers. They taught me about conflict—or did they? No, they only modeled what they knew about conflict, and that too was limited. So, like you, I grew into adulthood generally unaware and unprepared to successfully deal with the complex and varied conflicts I would be facing.

In the earliest days of my professional work, I was a classroom teacher. Almost immediately, I realized that the educational methods courses taught at the university failed to show me how I was to help my students work more effectively with one another. The classroom became my real-life laboratory to learn more about conflict. Add to this my role as wife and mother. Conflicts between my children, in my marriage, and between career and home responsibilities taught me a lot.

My attention on conflict became more focused as I next worked with many school districts in Michigan who were struggling with social change. Attempts to create equity in race, gender, and ethnicity were pushing educators away from old, comfortable ways into new cultural diversity. As an external consultant, I assisted them in solving both interpersonal and organizational conflicts.

My interest in conflict never waned as I expanded my training and consulting with business, hospitals, financial institutions, nonprofit organizations, and educational institutions. However, in all of these personal and professional activities, I was always searching for materials, both print and on-print, to help me assist others in dealing with conflict. I'd find a lone activity or two in various training handbooks, organization development books, and humanistic educational materials, but I never found what I needed most—a comprehensive handbook of training materials to use in my workshops and programs.

I decided the solution to this conflict was to write the book myself. After making this decision, I encountered several additional conflicts; for instance, should I merely collect all activities written by others under one cover? I decided against this strategy since each activity I located came from its own narrow perspective and was written in various forms. So I developed a frame of reference from which all activities would flow. The result was the Conflict Cycle, activities grouped under similar headings covering all aspects of conflict, and a format that was consistent and ready for immediate use. I was able to adapt some existing materials, however most of the activities in this handbook are original.

My final conflict was to decide when to stop writing. Just when I thought I had enough activities, I would think of another. Fortunately for you, I did stop or you wouldn't have this copy in your hands today. However, I do not intend to stop collecting, adapting, and writing—so this book will grow as we all learn from conflict.

Live Life Fully
Face Conflict
Teach Others
and
Learn From Conflict

Lyons, Colorado   L. B. H.
November 1980

Introduction

The training and development profession is growing rapidly. In some organizations, new departments are added that previously had little training beyond that of a technical nature. Existing departments are expanding. More people are receiving formal degrees in areas such as organizational behavior and human resource development. Many others who had a proven record as a supervisor or manager have become "instant" trainers for their organizations, learning process skills, adult learning theories, program design, and evaluation while "on the job." Both groups look to special programs and resource materials to provide them with practical ideas that could be used in their own instructional setting.

This book was written to meet the needs of trainers and instructors in a specific content area—*conflict*. Are you someone who is in a position to facilitate others who are learning from conflict? Perhaps you are an internal trainer serving your organization, or you're an external consultant working with many types of groups and organizations, or perhaps you teach in a public institution.

If you teach or instruct others, this book of instructional activities on conflict is for you. It is intended to offer a comprehensive set of materials on conflict.

1

Learning from Conflict
Why, What, and How?

Why is the topic of conflict so important? Conflict, as old as time, is everywhere. We do not have to look far to see conflicts on an interpersonal level, within our organizations, or in our nation and internationally. We also observe a variety of reactions to conflict and a range of personal styles that may or may not produce desired results. Thus, it is imperative that each of us, in our individual training and teaching capacities, use these positions to help others learn more about conflict, the kinds of conflicts engaged in, their causes, patterns of reaction, and methods to prevent and resolve conflicts.

A Definition

What is the definition of conflict? Simply stated, individuals or groups are in conflict when one or both parties are not obtaining what they need or want and are actively seeking their own end goal.

For example, in a negotiation process, the labor team is in conflict with the management team when labor persists in requesting a cost of living index and management insists it cannot grant such an inflationary provision. Both know what they want in the end, i.e., labor to receive more money and management to keep costs down. Even if they reach a settlement, the conflict may still exist because of unresolved issues or dissatisfaction with the contract. Until both parties are satisfied, conflict will remain.

A second example explaining this definition is a female employee wanting to adjust her work hours to correspond with those of her child's day care center. Her employer prefers to maintain a consistent procedure of work hours and avoid other employees' requests for flexible hours. The successful resolution of the conflict would be if both the employee and employer could establish a plan whereby the employee's work hours would include those prime hours when she must be available to other employees and customers they serve. The plan would include identifying others in the organization who need or desire flexible work hours. In this particular case both parties would satisfy their individual goals while resolving the basic conflict. This example fulfills the definition of a resolved conflict. Neither the employer nor the employee needs to actively continue pursuing what each wants.

The Conflict Cycle

The human organism knows it will have conflicts—it's a part of living. Conflict goes through a cycle of phases as shown in Figure 1-1. The first phase, anticipation, may be unconscious ("I think I'll wear my suit of armor just in case I get attacked.") or planned ("There's a likely candidate to have a conflict with."). We may have cues that conflicts are emerging—a grim face on our boss, sharp comments from a colleague, or other indicators of a brewing storm.

At some point, we move out of our turtle-like position, stick our necks out and become aware of a conflict. During the second phase we are like a hawk, flying around the

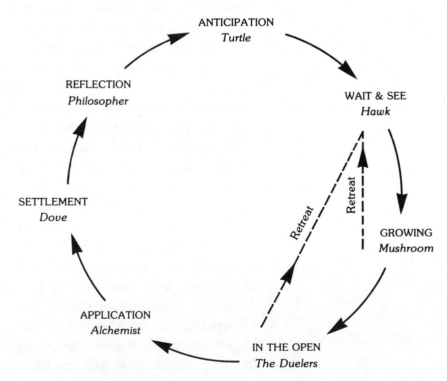

Figure 1-1. THE CONFLICT CYCLE

event and characters, gathering information, and trying to determine what to do next. For some period of time, we will wait and see what will happen.

However, unless the cause of the conflict is removed, it will mushroom, perhaps slowly, perhaps at an accelerated pace. By now we know it's not going to go away, even if we wish it would. What was small becomes bigger, and what was once avoidable is now unavoidable.

Now the conflict is in the open. Sides are taken, issues are clearer, tension is high, and defenses are up. At this point, we might choose to take a temporary retreat to the wait-and-see position with appeasement, denial, or suppression. Eventually, we must reemerge into the open, but for now we hold off. A second route is to press on.

The next phase is applying a method, or combination of methods, to resolve the conflict. Such as an alchemist faces, finding the right formula to fit the problem may require several attempts. A settlement is reached when all those involved are satisfied. A truce is called, tension is dissipated, and energies are redirected into other activities. Like cooing doves, the parties in conflict might recapture earlier feelings of affection toward one another.

A key part of the cycle is the reflection stage. This phase permits those involved in the conflict to philosophically ask questions such as, "What did I learn about myself, others, and this organization?" or "What did I do that I'm proud of?" or "What would I do differently if I could replay this scenario?"

The reflection phase is so important and yet is often forgotten or ignored. If the individuals involved in the conflict completed the other phases and reached a settlement, but did not make the effort to analyze what was learned, most likely the attitudes and behaviors of each would remain the same when engaged in their next conflict. If, however, each of those involved reevaluated the appropriateness of their own behavior, more likely the next conflict would be resolved more easily and with a higher level of satisfaction. Each would have truly learned from conflict.

Constructive vs. Destructive Aspects of Conflict

During the reflective phase, we can also analyze both the constructive and destructive aspects of conflict. Both do exist to differing degrees. As the trainer or instructor, you need to review both aspects. One way is to recall some conflicts you have been personally involved in and list some ways in which you and others were negatively and positively affected. Here are some possibilities.

Conflict Is Destructive When It:

- Diverts energy from more important activities and issues
- Destroys the morale of people or reinforces poor self-concepts
- Polarizes groups so they increase internal cohesiveness and reduces intergroup cooperation
- Deepens differences in values
- Produces irresponsible and regrettable behavior such as name-calling and fighting.

Conflict Is Constructive When It:

- Opens up issues of importance, resulting in their clarification
- Results in the solution of problems
- Increases the involvement of individuals in issues of importance to them
- Causes authentic communication to occur
- Serves as a release to pent-up emotion, anxiety and stress
- Helps build cohesiveness among people by sharing the conflict, celebrating in its settlement and learning more about each other
- Helps individuals grow personally and apply what they learned to future situations.

As the group leader, you must be as clear as possible as to your view of conflict. Is your intent to present the position that conflict is always destructive and should be avoided at all costs? Or, will you offer the polarities? Hopefully, you will find the balance between, offering participants the opportunity to learn and grow from conflict.

A second clarification activity for you to experience, and then help participants do the same, is to be aware of how people learn attitudes toward conflict and the styles of dealing with them.

Messages About Conflict: How did we learn about conflict? Growing up, few of us were given school courses on conflict. Some were told how to fight the neighborhood bully, but mostly, we learned about conflict by observing others around us. What messages were you taught? Do any of these sound familiar?

"Don't pick a fight, but if you're in one, win it!"
"Fighting never solved anything!"
"Girls don't fight!"
"Never hit a girl!"
"Bite your tongue."
"If you haven't anything nice to say, don't say anything at all."
"Turn the other cheek."
"An eye for an eye . . ."

These messages were based on the values, attitudes, and experiences of our parents, teachers, church, and community. They varied according to our religion, race, ethnicity, and gender. They carried strong meanings; thus, each of us carries around our own beliefs, assumptions, and behavioral styles about how we will face and resolve conflict.

The participants in your training programs will also hold their own set of beliefs and assumptions. They will demonstrate their own unique style of dealing with conflict, based on their unique set of life experiences. You can help them explore their "childhood messages" and current beliefs about conflict by using activities found in Chapter 2.

The challenge for you as a trainer or instructor is to present programs or workshops that help participants look positively upon conflict so they will *learn* from conflicts. Rather than learning that conflict is inevitable, normal, and manageable, their experiences in life may have taught them that conflict is dangerous, disruptive, and useless. As long as people are different, holding different opinions, values, and knowledge, each group and organization will have conflicts.

Assumptions

We have explored the meaning of conflict, its effects, the phases of the conflict cycle, and how we learned our conflict styles. The following section will provide the assumptions upon which this book was written. They are as follows:

1. Conflicts and disagreements will develop. It is how we understand, resolve, and learn from them that is important.

2. Some conflicts can be minimized. Applying ideas and methods in this book can help people to prevent conflicts from ballooning into unnecessary and less manageable sizes.

3. There are some unavoidable conflicts, ones that shouldn't be smoothed over or suppressed. These can be resolved, applying many of the methods and ideas found here.

4. The resolution of conflict does not have to result in a winner or a loser. There are methods we can use to help those involved solve the problem in a manner that is not done at the expense of others' integrity, and everyone involved is a winner.

Book's Organization

The next seven chapters detail the fundamentals of this book. Chapter 2, *Getting Started,* provides activities to "warm-up" the group and introduce them to the topic of conflict. Chapter 3, *Naming,* has activities to help participants identify the kinds of conflicts in which they are involved. Chapter 4, *Reacting,* includes activities to explore the variety of ways people react to conflicts. Chapter 5, *Searching,* includes activities that explore causes of conflicts: differences based on perceptions, assumptions, expectations, values, wants and needs, knowledge, culture, gender, and age. Chapter 6, *Preventing,* includes some ways to prevent the escalation of conflicts. Chapter 7, *Resolving,* has activities to help people find resolution to conflicts. Chapter 8,

Planning for Conflict, consists of activities for participants to summarize their learning and plan for future action.

The structured activities fall into three types. First, there are some that help individuals focus on themselves, increasing their knowledge of their styles of reacting to and resolving conflicts. Second, some activities focus on interpersonal conflicts between two individuals, or perhaps within a small group. Third, some activities focus on intergroup conflicts.

Each activity is presented with the same format, beginning with the background information. This includes the objectives, group size, amount of time required, and materials to be utilized. Then, the steps of the process are outlined, and worksheets for participants plus special comments or suggestions for variations follow. Since the objectives of activities overlap between the seven sections, a cross-reference to other activities is included. Appropriate references are also listed.

The Planning Process

For a successful workshop in conflict, careful planning is essential. Planning an event such as this involves tasks in seven areas: program, arrangements, promotion, displays, fiscal, evaluation, and registration.[1] Naturally, if you are running a one-person show, the responsibility for these tasks may feel awesome. If, however, you have other trainers and support personnel to assist you with many of these tasks, you may be sharing the load of overall responsibility, but must monitor the planning process.

Since this book consists of activities for programs on conflict, the discussion that follows will focus on that one area of planning—program development. The following briefly outlines five important steps:[2]

[1]For a comprehensive list of all the administrative tasks needed to set up a workshop, see Lois B. Hart and Gordon Schleicher, *A Conference and Workshop Planners' Manual* (New York: AMACOM, American Management Associations, 1979).
[2]For more complete directions on program design and evaluation, read Larry Davis and Earl McCallon, *Planning, Conducting and Evaluating Workshops* (Austin, Texas: Learning Concepts, 1974).

1. Diagnose participants' readiness and needs. This crucial step should be taken well before you plan the program's design. What do the participants know about conflict? What kinds of conflicts do they face regularly in their organizations and personal lives? Why would they want to take time to attend your program? How is it in their self-interest? What other programs have been offered on the topic of conflict or other topics that would mesh well with this planned program? What support is there from the organization's decision makers to conduct this program?

2. Design the program. The sequence of activities in your program will depend on what you have learned in the diagnosis. Keep in mind your participants' past experiences and knowledge, how well they know each other, how much time is available, and the possibility of follow-up. Write your objectives. Should they include objectives from all seven sections—getting started, naming, reacting, search, preventing, and resolving? Or are your goals, and thus your objectives, to focus on only one aspect of the topic?

With your objectives in one hand and this collection of activities in the other, review the activities. As you read, keep in mind that people who are work-related (those who work together regularly), or people who are strangers (those who come to the program unfamiliar with one another), may have little knowledge or previous training in conflict. Therefore, they may need activities that are nonthreatening. Always work from a low-threat level to a more intensive one.

In selecting activities, remember that they were written with many types of groups in mind. Therefore, no activity, as written, will fit your needs perfectly. Adapt, modify, and mix and match as best fits your needs. (Sample designs for programs of varying lengths are included at the end of this chapter.) Once you have picked the activities for your program's design, applying your most important criteria, let the design rest. After a few days, review your objectives and activities and determine if the flow of the design still makes sense. You can also ask a sample of prospective participants and/or other colleagues for their opinion of the general design.

3. Establish staffing plan. Will you present the program alone? Would it be appropriate or possible to team up with someone else to present the program? If at all possible, training teams should closely match the experience, gender, race, and ethnic composition of the participants' group.

Whoever serves as the trainer(s) should be thoroughly familiar with the organization in which the program will be presented. They should also be well acquainted with the goal and objectives, activities and materials, and with whomever they will share this responsibility.

4. Try it out. All program designs need to be flexible to meet emerging needs of participants; trainers also need to flow with the tide. If a planned activity is not working, find out why, then adapt it or drop it if necessary. Continually seek feedback from the participants. Record modifications you made, and reactions and comments to activities you use from this book.

Sample Training Designs

It may be helpful for you to consider some training designs used with a variety of groups. The following examples are designs used for a short three-hour session, or a one-day, three-day, or week-long workshop. Almost all the designs incorporate activities from the next seven chapters. Of course, the longer designs allow for time to explore more aspects of conflict and in greater depth.

Remember, these are only samples; you need to develop your program design based on the needs of your own group of participants.

Notes to Myself

Three-Hour Design

Objectives
- To draw the phases of the conflict cycle
- To review typical conflicts in which one is involved, possible causes and methods generally used
- To distinguish between five methods of resolving conflicts

Time	Category	Activities	Chapter	Pages
30 min.	Getting Started	-Review objectives -Conflict Cycle -Assumptions	2	27
2 hours	Naming, Reacting, Searching, Resolving	-Conflict Chart	3	43
30 min.	Planning for Conflict	-Summary -I Learned . . . -Evaluation	8	205

Notes to Myself

One-Day Design

Objectives
- To draw the phases of the conflict cycle
- To trace some causes of conflict to differing perceptions and expectations
- To name some recent conflicts and how one reacted to each
- To select variables in one's organization that both help and hinder the development and resolution of conflict
- To distinguish between five methods of resolving conflict
- To select one's own level of self-interest to resolve conflicts

Time	Category	Activities	Chapter	Pages
9:00	Getting Started	-Introduce facilitator(s) -Is Conflict Destructive or Constructive? -Conflict Cycle -Assumptions -Review of workshop objectives and agenda	2 1,2 1	35 27
	Searching	-How Many Do You See? -What Do You See? -Expectations: Mine and Theirs	5 5 5	97 103 115
	Naming	-Conflict Chart	3	43
	Reacting	-It's in the Body	4	71
12:00	Lunch Break			
1:15	Preventing	-Checking on the Climate	6	131
2:30	Resolving	-Five Methods of Resolving Conflict -Self-Interest	7 7	179 151
	Summary/Evaluation	-Review conflict cycle, objectives, plans of action -Evaluation	8	

Notes to Myself

Three-Day Design

Objectives

- To draw the phases of the conflict cycle
- To name patterns of conflicts in which one has been engaged
- To identify one's pattern of reacting to conflicts
- To trace some causes of conflicts to differing values, wants, perceptions, and expectations
- To select variables in one's organization that both help and hinder the development and resolution of conflict
- To distinguish between five methods of resolving conflicts
- To learn and practice resolution methods of identifying self-interest, rules for fighting, listening skills, measuring intensity of a conflict, and problem solving
- To adapt one's style for future conflicts through practice sessions in role playing and fishbowling

Time	Category	Activities	Chapter	Pages
Day 1				
A.M.	Getting Started	-Introduce facilitator(s)		
		-Is Conflict Destructive or Constructive?	2	35
		-Conflict Cycle	1,2	27
		-Assumptions	1	
		-Review workshop objectives and agenda		
		-Childhood Messages	2	29
	Naming	-Conflict Chart	3	43
		-Conflict in the Hat	3	49
Lunch Break				
P.M.	Reacting	-It's in the Body	4	71
		-What Is Your Conflict Style?	4	77
Day 2				
A.M.	Searching	-My Values, Your Values, and Our Values	5	91
		-Want in a Hat	5	89

Time	Category	Activities	Chapter	Pages
Day 2				
A.M.		-Perceptions:	5	
		1. How Many Do You See?		97
		2. Connect the Dots		99
		3. What Do You See?		103
Lunch Break				
P.M.	Searching (cont.)	-Expectations: Mine and Theirs	5	115
	Preventing	-Checking on the Climate	6	131
Day 3	Resolving	-Five Methods of Resolving		
A.M.	(Interpersonal)	Conflict	7	179
		-Self-Interest	7	151
		-Fighting Fairly	7	163
		-Tell Me and I'll Listen	7	167
		-Act it Out	7	173
		-Conflict Scale	7	159
Lunch Break				
P.M.	Resolving	-The Fishbowl	7	189
	(Organizational)	-Compact Problem-Solving		
		Process	7	193
	Summary/Evaluation	-Review conflict cycle,		
		objectives, plan of action	7	
		-Evaluation	8	

Five-Day Design

Objectives
- To identify both the constructive and destructive aspects of conflict
- To draw the phases of the conflict cycle
- To name the messages learned in childhood about conflict
- To name patterns of conflicts in which one has been engaged personally and in one's organization
- To identify one's pattern of reacting to conflicts
- To determine aspects of one's style that needs changing
- To trace some causes of conflicts to differing values, wants, assumptions, knowledge, perceptions, and expectations
- To select variables in one's organization that both help and hinder the development and resolution of conflict
- To uncover conflicts that are suppressed
- To distinguish between five methods of resolving conflicts
- To learn and practice resolution methods of identifying self-interest, rules for fighting, listening skills, measuring intensity of a conflict, and problem solving
- To adapt one's style for future conflicts through practice sessions in role playing and fishbowling
- To develop an individual plan for dealing with future conflicts

Time	Category	Activities	Chapter	Pages
Pre-Workshop	Assignment	-Send instructions to participants for them to complete before the workshop		
		a. For the Record	3	
		b. A Weekly Record	3	
Day 1 A.M.	Getting Started	-Introduce facilitator(s)		
		-Conflict Means . . .	2	31
		-Is Conflict Destructive or Constructive?	2	35
		-Conflict Cycle	1,2	27

Time	Category	Activities	Chapter	Pages
Day 1 A.M.	Getting Started	–Assumptions	1	
		–Review of workshop objectives and agenda		
		–Childhood Messages	2	29
		–Conflict Opinionnaire	2	
P.M.	Naming	–For the Record and Weekly Record	3	51,55
		–Conflict Chart	3	43
		–Searching for Patterns of Organizational Conflict	3	61
		–Imaging	3	59
Day 2	Reacting	–What Is Your Conflict Style?	4	77
		–It's in the Body	4	71
		–Sculpting	4	75
		–Feelings Collage	4	79
		–Selling One's Style of Conflict	4	81
Day 3	Searching	–My Values, Your Values, and Our Values	5	91
		–Want in a Hat	5	89
		–Do You Know What I Know?	5	111
		–Perceptions:	5	
		1. How Many Do You See?		97
		2. Connect the dots		99
		3. What Do You See?	5	103
		–Testing Our Assumptions	5	107
		–Expectations: Mine and Theirs	5	115
Day 4 A.M.	Preventing	–Checking on the Climate	6	131
		–Gunnysacking: The Garbage Pail	6	137
P.M.	Resolving	–Five Methods of Resolving Conflict	7	179
		–Self-Interest	7	151
		–Fighting Fairly	7	163
Day 5	Resolving (cont'd.)	–Tell Me and I'll Listen	7	167
		–Act it Out	7	173
		–Conflict Scale	7	159
		–The Fishbowl	7	189
		–Compact Problem-Solving Process	7	193
	Summary and Follow-up	–Summarize conflict cycle, major points		
		–Develop individual plans for action	8	
	Evaluation			

Helping Others
In your role as a trainer, instructor, or teacher, you have the opportunity to help others expand their knowledge about conflict, their ability to face conflicts, and most important, to learn from conflicts.

This chapter has provided the foundation—a definition of conflict, the identification of phases of conflicts, an understanding of both the destructive and constructive aspects of conflict, and the clarification of assumptions underlying the purpose of this book. Upon this foundation is the framework of the book—an explanation of the process of planning programs on conflict and sample designs.

Within this framework are the distinct and yet interchangeable tools or parts of the design, including getting the group started, naming conflicts, searching for causes, identifying how one reacts to various conflicts, utilizing methods of preventing and resolving conflicts, and developing plans for facing future conflicts. These tools are the numerous activities found in the following chapters.

You now have the foundation, framework, and tools to build meaningful programs to help others *learn from conflict.*

Notes to Myself

2

Getting Started

When facing a new group of participants, the trainer has the initial challenge of getting their attention. Each person walks in the door with pressing problems, unsolved decisions, piles of work remaining on his or her desk, unanswered phone calls, and personal errands not done. To add to this, each individual has a personal set of values, expectations, and experiences that predetermine the degree of interest in the workshop. Unfortunately, what these people carry into the workshop may not be easy to decipher. If the trainer ignores the individuals' "baggage," learning may be delayed, distorted, and limited. So, one purpose of introductory or warm-up activities, in any workshop, is to prepare the learners for the experience ahead, and to help them separate themselves from the other issues, demands, and aspects of their lives long enough to immerse themselves into the planned program.

The second purpose of such introductory activities is to provide the foundation for the planned workshop to clarify concepts, terms, and underlying assumptions, and to establish the frame of reference for the experience. Without these elements present, participants may wonder throughout the program why they are there, why they remain confused as to the meaning of the topic, and why they are uncertain about the direction in which they are heading.

The purpose of this chapter is to provide activities that will get the participants' attention, and also provide the foundation and framework for the program. You may have noted that each of the sample designs in Chapter 1 included one or several of these activities, and each included an explanation of the conflict cycle.

Notes to Myself

The Conflict Cycle

Objectives To recognize the phases of the conflict cycle

Group Size Any size

Time Required Thirty minutes to one hour

Materials Utilized Transparency or copy of the Conflict Cycle (Figure 1-1) for each participant

Physical Setting Classroom style, facing front of room

Content and Process

1. Introduce the purpose and objective of learning about the conflict cycle.

2. Provide a visual representation of the cycle, using either a copy or transparency of Figure 1-1.

3. Using the information provided on the conflict cycle and its phases (found in Chapter 1), review each phase of the cycle, providing numerous examples.

4. Relate the *reflection* phase of the conflict cycle to the basic assumptions and purpose of this workshop; that is, to learn from conflict. Specific objectives and agenda for the workshop are explained, discussed, and agreed upon.

Variations/ Comments Participants, in trios or small groups, can trace a conflict they went through recently, following the phases of the conflict cycle.

Notes to Myself

Childhood Messages

Objectives   To name the *messages* we learned about conflict as we were growing up

Group Size   Groups of three

Time Required   Thirty minutes to one hour

Materials Utilized   Newsprint or chalkboard

Physical Setting   Moveable chairs to form small groups

Content and Process

    1. Introduce the concept of *messages*. Explain the objectives of the activity.

    2. In groups of three, discuss and list the key messages around conflict that each person learned from parents, teachers, peers, church, etc., while they were growing up.

    3. In the total group, share these messages, making a list on newsprint or the chalkboard. They may include the following:

"Don't pick a fight, but if you're in one, win it!"

"Fighting never solved anything!"

"Girls don't fight!"

"Never hit a girl!"

"Bite your tongue."

"If you haven't anything nice to say, don't say anything at all."

"Turn the other cheek."

"An eye for an *eye* . . ."

    4. Ask the group the following questions, then discuss their answers.

      a. Which of these messages dominate how you feel about conflicts today?

      b. Which messages will you discard or modify?

      c. Which messages will you retain?

5. Relate the value of naming childhood messages to the purpose of this workshop.

Variations/ Comments

Have a participant act out one of those people who taught the messages. For instance, have one participant become the parent or teacher and "teach" the message to another participant, who should react as a child might. Replay the scene with the "child," choosing another reaction.

Cross-Reference Activities

1. Is Conflict Destructive or Constructive? (this chapter)
2. Growing Up (Chapter 5)
3. Act it Out (Chapter 7)

Conflict Means . . .

Objectives To identify the connotations of the word *conflict*

Group Size Groups of three

Time Required Thirty minutes to one hour

Materials Utilized One copy of the worksheet, Conflict Means . . ., for each person

Content and Process

1. Introduce the definition of *connotation*.
   a. Call out a word, such as *love, honor,* or *loyalty,* and ask for the first thought(s) that come to mind. Note how many different responses there are.
   b. Define *connotation* as "the suggestive significance of a word apart from its explicit and recognized meaning."
   c. Explain the objective of this activity.
2. Form groups of three. Give each participant the worksheet and ask all group members to give their immediate reaction to each word on the list, and to list other words that connotate its meaning. After they have identified their reactions, have the participants discuss:
   a. Which words produced the strongest positive emotional reaction?
   b. Which words produced the strongest negative emotional reaction?
   c. What synonyms they listed.
   d. Why they think they reacted the way they did.
   e. How they learned to react that way.
3. Have a discussion with the total group, drawing upon the above questions. Relate how these words interrelate with the word *conflict*. Define conflict as explained in Chapter 1: "Conflict exists when one or both parties are not obtaining what they need or want and are actively seeking their own goals."

| **Variations/** | Add or delete words in the worksheet. Read the list of |
| **Comments** | words to the total group and quickly list all reactions. |

| **Cross-Reference** | Childhood Messages (this chapter) |
| **Activity** | |

Conflict Means . . .

Directions   As you read each word in the left column, note your immediate emotional, or gut-level, reaction and put a check mark in the column that most closely matches your reaction.

In the far right column, list other words that come to your mind.

Words	Reactions					Connotations
	Strongly positive	**Somewhat positive**	**Neutral**	**Somewhat negative**	**Strongly negative**	
Conflict						
Compromise						
Authority						
Resolutions						
Problem solving						
Confront						
Power						
Tension						
Collaboration						

Notes to Myself

Is Conflict Destructive or Constructive?

Objectives   To identify both the destructive and constructive outcomes of conflict

Group Size   Any size, if presented as a lecturette; otherwise, divide into groups of five to seven people

Time Required   Thirty minutes to one hour

Materials Utilized   Transparencies of key aspects (one for destructive and one for constructive), newsprint, and markers for each group

Physical Setting   Classroom setting facing front with flexibility to form small groups

Content and Process

1. Open with the statement, "We all have our beliefs about the value of conflict—some believe conflict is basically destructive, and some believe that it can be constructive." Review the objective of this activity.

2. Have the small groups make a list on newsprint of all the destructive outcomes of conflict and a second list of all of the constructive outcomes of conflict. Suggest that individuals keep in mind actual conflicts they have experienced so that they can more easily name both aspects of conflict. Have one person in each group record the group's ideas.

3. Have the small groups give their reports, summarizing the lists and posting them on the wall. (You may want to show your lists from Chapter 1, "Constructive vs. Destructive Aspects of Conflict," on some transparencies for possible ideas.)

4. Discuss:

a. What happens if our beliefs about conflict being destructive outnumber our beliefs about the constructive aspects of conflict?

b. How did we obtain these beliefs?

c. Which beliefs can we give up easily?

d. Which beliefs must we modify if we accept the assumption of this workshop; that is, we can learn from conflict?

Variations/ Comments   If time is limited, you could omit the small group work and present a lecturette about both aspects of conflict.

Cross-Reference Activities   1. The Conflict Cycle (this chapter)
2. Childhood Messages (this chapter)

Conflict Continuum

Objectives

1. To prepare participants for more in-depth exploration of personal conflicts
2. To identify how one generally reacts to conflict

Group Size

Any size, if done as a written activity; groups of ten to fifteen, if done as a continuum where people stand

Time Required

Forty-five minutes to one hour

Materials Utilized

None

Physical Setting

Large enough room for a line of people

Content and Process

1. Present the following continuum (shown in the diagram below) of two extreme types of people. Ask participants to determine where their general style of reacting to conflicts falls between these two extremes. Those who are writing their responses should place an X at a key point along the line. Those in groups of ten to fifteen people should form a line, representing the different styles of reacting to conflict, with the extremes marked at either end of the room.

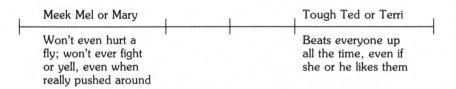

Meek Mel or Mary			Tough Ted or Terri
Won't even hurt a fly; won't ever fight or yell, even when really pushed around			Beats everyone up all the time, even if she or he likes them

2. Discuss with participants why they marked or chose that particular spot. They can give examples of how they react behaviorally to conflict, and how it serves their purposes to behave that way.

3. After this discussion, have participants put another check mark on the line, or change their position in line, to

indicate how they would prefer to react to conflict. Asking the participants the following questions may be useful:

    a. Is there a difference between your actual position on the continuum and your desired position?

    b. If there is a difference, what stops you from getting to your desired position?

    c. Imagine a time when you have acted in your actual positions. How did you feel then?

    d. Have you ever acted in your desired position? How did you feel?

Their answers may be written, discussed in small groups, or discussed in the whole group.

3

Naming

The key element to increasing choices for preventing and resolving conflicts is *naming*. Naming conflicts involves an honest and in-depth identification of areas of conflicts, patterns of when they occur, how often, and with whom. Because this step can be time-consuming and painful, especially when it uncovers that which we had hoped to suppress, the naming process is often glossed over and even skipped. Common responses are, "Oh, I know what the problem is so I won't waste my time on this step," or "We've studied the problem already in committee; let's get on to solutions."

Thus, the wise trainer, instructor, and teacher will watch for resistance, on their part and the part of their participants, to move too quickly through the naming stage. If activities are chosen that are unique approaches to naming conflicts, different from methods the participants commonly use, then some resistance may be overcome.

The point here is that there is value in naming conflicts. It can uncover that which was avoided or suppressed. It can be preventive medicine, allowing for discussion of conflicts before they reach an exaggerated stage. Stated even more succinctly, "to name it is to claim it." Once a conflict is named, the hardest step toward resolution has occurred. It is no longer elusive or intangible, but more manageable.

There are three possible outcomes of this chapter's activities on naming. First, patterns of conflicts can be identified. Isolated incidents do not cause recurring conflicts. If, however, similar types of conflicts occur with the same type of person, or conflicts at similar times are observed, then the namers can also apply resolution methods that best fit the described patterns. Second, the naming process gets the conflict into the open, leads to acceptance of its existence, and opens up interest in doing something about it. Third, naming facilitates clarification of the issues or problems. A well-defined problem is much easier to resolve.

The following activities attempt to name patterns of conflicts. Some focus on interpersonal conflicts while others look

at intergroup and intraorganizational conflicts. The naming
process can occur at the time of the workshop or over a
period of time before and during the learning process.

Conflict Chart
Looking for Patterns and Choices

Objectives

1. To name conflicts one has recently had with several types of people
2. To identify sources of conflict for individuals
3. To identify methods used by individual and group members to resolve conflict
4. To explore how we learn about conflict resolution techniques
5. To learn the difference between "Win/Lose" and "Win/Win"

Group Size

A variety is used as described below

Time Required

One to three hours (This activity can be used completely for a three-hour design, or used partially in conjunction with other activities.)

Materials Utilized

A Conflict Chart per person (See the worksheet at the end of this activity.)

Physical Setting

Desks and chairs grouped together

Content and Process

1. Introduce the lesson in one of these ways:
a. Show an excerpt from a film that shows a conflict.
b. Post several pictures showing different forms of conflict.
c. Role play with a participant who likes to act, simulating a conflict between you and that person.
d. Introduce the concept of *gaming*—conflict having a winner and a loser.

Use one of these dramatic introductions as a means of getting the participants' attention. Ask, "What is conflict?

How do we get ourselves involved in conflict? How do we resolve our conflict? How do you feel when you see conflict? How do you feel when you experience a conflict?" Explain objectives of this activity.

2. Pass out the Conflict Chart worksheet to each person. Each person fills in her or his own chart without any help. It is important that there be no talking at this point so that everyone has a chance to think about their own situation without interference. Give the following instructions for each section of the chart:

a. *Person*

In this column list types of persons with whom you come in contact. As you look the list over, think about a particular person in each category until you are "seeing" that person in your mind. Add any other type that has been left out and with whom you interact regularly.

b. *Cause of Conflict*

Next to each person's name, briefly write down conflicts you have had with that person in the past. What was the conflict about? (It is all right not to fill in everyone, but do at least half of the names.)

c. *Methods*

Next, recall what happened with each case of conflict. What did you do and what did the other person do? The goal here is to list the *methods* used by both of you in trying to resolve the conflict.

d. *Who Won?*

Think about the concept of gaming, introduced earlier. Recall each conflict situation and decide who won. Put a check mark in the appropriate column under "Who Won?"

3. The objective of this next part is to share information about sources and methods of conflict resolution. Form groups of four to five people, and select or assign someone to record the information. It is suggested that each point be covered as a unit before going on to the next one. Thus,

each group will complete the first question, report to the total group, and then go on to the next question.

a. *Sources*

Have individuals list all causes of conflict that they have experienced. (Later activities found in Chapter 5 on *Searching* can be used.) Present the following questions:

Do the causes fall into any particular patterns?
How many causes are from within the individual?
How many causes are from outside sources?
What type of person do you have the most conflict with?

b. *Feelings*

How do you feel when you have conflicts with others?
Does one type of conflict cause a stronger reaction than others?

c. *Methods*

Each person should then list all of the methods they experienced, and ask themselves if the methods fall into any particular categories. Have them code each method individually, using the following key, according to where they learned these methods:

UN = Unknown   P = from Peers
PA = from parents   T = Television/Movies

As a group, ask the participants to count up each of the codes and give a total number for each. (This should reveal to them that generally we are not formally taught how to deal with conflict, and that we often learn methods from the example of others! See Childhood Messages (Chapter 2).)

d. *Who Won?*

Participants should then look at their own sheets, add up each column in this section, and ask themselves how satisfied they are with the results they are getting from the methods they are currently using to resolve conflict. Count up the number of wins and losses in the columns. What does this tell us?

e. *Goal Setting*

Next, ask each person to reflect on the following (either by thinking about it or by writing out an answer): Look over the list of methods. Select five which you would never consider using. Select five which you have never tried or used infrequently, but would consider trying. Select from this list those possibilities that you will try the next time you are having a conflict with others. Write down a contract to yourself: I _____ will use the following method of resolving conflict _____ the very next time I have the opportunity. Think about what would keep you from trying out a new method of resolving conflict?

Note: this is for each participant's own use and should be kept confidential.

Variations/ Comments   You may decide to have participants complete only certain parts of the chart at a time, stopping to expand on its particular content. For example, you may ask them to perform item 3a, listing sources of conflict. Then some in-depth activities found in the chapter on *Searching* may be presented.

Cross-Reference Activities   1. All activities on *Searching* (Chapter 5)
2. All activities on *Resolving* (Chapter 7)

Conflict Chart for General Use

Person	Causes of Conflict	Methods Used		Who Won?			
		By Me	By Other(s)	I Did	They Did	We Both Won	We Both Lost
Stranger							
Acquaintance							
Close friend							
Spouse							
Own child							
Own parent							
Boss							
Colleague							
Subordinate							
Client/Customer							

Notes to Myself

Conflict in the Hat

Objectives

1. To name conflict situations
2. To promote self-disclosure of one's feelings and attitudes about conflict

Group Size

Up to ten per group

Time Required

Forty-five minutes to one hour

Materials Utilized

3″ × 5″ cards, and hats or empty boxes

Physical Setting

A circle of chairs for each group

Content and Process

1. Tell each person to complete this sentence on a 3″ × 5″ card: "You will find me in the midst of a conflict when . . ."

2. Collect the cards and shuffle them inside a hat or box. Each person then picks a new card from the hat.

3. One at a time, have the participants read their new card and then complete this sentence: "I imagine that this person . . ."

4. After all cards are read and responded to by the readers, discuss conflict with the group, using these questions:

    a. How did you feel hearing your conflict read and discussed by another person?

    b. How did you feel hearing about other people's conflicts?

    c. What patterns did you notice?

Variations / Comments

Select additional incomplete sentences to respond to, such as:

    "A recent conflict I had was . . ."

    "The basic issue was . . ."

Cross-Reference Activities

1. All activities on *Reacting* (Chapter 4)
2. All activities on *Searching* (Chapter 5)

For the Record

Objectives
1. To record incidents of conflict in our lives
2. To search for patterns of causes of conflict
3. To identify resolution methods we generally use

Group Size
Any number

Time Required
Ten days, generally over a two-week period

Materials Utilized
A copy of the worksheet For the Record Log Sheet for each participant

Physical Setting
Tables and chairs

Content and Process

1. Once a day, for ten days, instruct each participant to record at least one conflict he or she had that day with someone else. Use the code found on the log sheet to identify with whom the conflict occurred. This information is recorded for a period of two weeks.

2. After the chart is filled up, ask each person to review the information and respond to these questions:
   a. With whom did you have the most conflicts? With whom did you have the least number of conflicts?
   b. What were most of your conflicts about?
   c. List the methods you used to resolve your conflicts. Which method(s) were used the most, and which were used the least? How successful do you think your methods were?
   d. Complete each of these sentences:
      "I learned that I . . ."
      "I wonder why I . . ."
      "I plan to . ."

Variations/Comments
Participants may record incidents of conflict over a longer period of time.

Cross-Reference Activities

1. Conflict Chart (this chapter), which goes beyond identification of sources of conflict
2. All activities on *Searching* (Chapter 5), which may be used later
3. All activities on *Resolving* (Chapter 7), which may be used later

For the Record Log Sheet

Code	
Spouse/Intimate	Boss
Own Child	Co-worker
My Parent(s)	Stranger
Close Friend	Acquaintance
Client/Customer	Subordinate

	Conflict Was With:	Conflict Was About:	Conflict Was Resolved By:
Day 1			
Day 2			
Day 3			
Day 4			
Day 5			
Day 6			
Day 7			
Day 8			
Day 9			
Day 10			

Notes to Myself

A Weekly Record of Conflict

Objectives
1. To record incidents of conflict in one's life over a six-week period
2. To search for patterns in the causes and resolution of conflicts

Group Size Any size group can participate

Time Required Over a six-week period

Materials Utilized A copy of the worksheet accompanying this activity

Physical Setting Tables and chairs

Content and Process

1. Once a week, preferably at the end of the week, ask each person to privately complete a "Weekly Record of Conflict" worksheet. These should be dated and signed (a code number can be used for each person if anonymity is needed), and then collected and stored in a safe place. Or, if people prefer, they can file each sheet on their own.

2. At the end of six weeks, return each person's sheets from the previous weeks. Review them for the purpose of searching for patterns—What conflicts occur most frequently? With whom? How were they resolved? Which ones remain unresolved?

3. After this silent reflection period, create small groups to compare observations. It is important that each person's right to determine what information is shared is preserved. Later, ask each small group to report on the main points of their discussion to the total group.

4. Finally, ask each person to summarize what has been learned by completing these sentences:

"I learned that I . . ."
"I wonder why I . . ."
"I plan to . . ."

Variations / Comments

Questions on the worksheets can be adapted to fit the needs and interests of your particular participants.

Cross-Reference Activities

1. Conflict Chart (this chapter), which goes beyond the identification of the sources of one's conflicts
2. All activities on *Searching* (Chapter 5)
3. All activities on *Resolving* (Chapter 7)

A Weekly Record of Conflict

Name or code _____ Date _____

1. What was a conflict you had with yourself this week? Record some of the "inner dialogue" you had with yourself and what the final result was.

2. What was a conflict you had with your spouse, intimate, another relative, or one of your children? Explain what was behind the conflict and what happened.

3. Did you have any conflicts with anyone at work? With whom? What sparked the conflict? Who won the battle? Did others get involved?

Notes to Myself

Imaging
What Is the Conflict?

Objectives

1. To identify the nature of the relationship between two groups
2. To name the intergroup problems causing conflict

Group Size

Two small groups of six to eight people; one facilitator for every group

Time Required

One-half day for naming aspect, or more if resolution techniques are used also.

Materials Utilized

Newsprint, markers, tape, and a circle of chairs far enough apart to ensure privacy.

Content and Process

1. Introduce the objectives, guidelines, and process for the session.

2. Form groups based on their present differences or established work units.

3. Ask each group to write, on newsprint, images of:

a. their own group

b. the other group

The images are based on observed behaviors, both favorable and unfavorable. One sheet should be made for each kind. The facilitator for each small group should help the group remain focused and verify their images.

4. Reconvene the two groups. Arrange Group A in an inner circle while Group B posts their newsprint. As each item is read, have alternate members of Group A paraphrase what was said. (See Tell Me and I'll Listen (Chapter 7).)

5. Ask the groups to exchange places so that Group B paraphrases each item read to them by Group A.

6. Separate the two groups again. With the facilitators' help, ask each group to recall examples of their behavior that support both the favorable and unfavorable images provided by the other group.

7. Reconvene the two groups to share what new evidence was uncovered in the previous step.

8. The facilitators should then help the groups identify the key issues of their conflict with one another, and use one of the techniques found in Chapter 7, *Resolving.*

Variations/ Comments This exercise is useful when used as an introductory activity in a series of events. It can uncover suppressed conflicts, set the stage for problem solving, and utilize communication skills. (*See Resolving* (Chapter 7).) However, it must be done in a safe environment with established guidelines.

Cross-Reference Activity Tell Me and I'll Listen (Chapter 7)

Searching for Patterns of Organizational Conflict

Objectives:
1. To identify patterns of conflicts which occur in an organization
2. To seek some causes of persistent conflicts

Group Size
Members from various levels in the organizations can participate; one facilitator per ten participants is necessary

Time Required
Either hold a two- to three-hour workshop where individuals complete the information, or request they complete the form before attending

Materials Utilized
A copy of the worksheet accompanying this activity

Content and Process

1. Identify those who will participate in the collection of this information. Orient them to the purpose and procedures to be used.

2. Ask each person to complete the worksheet for this activity.

3. Form small groups (either homogeneous or heterogeneous) to share their observations. With the help of a facilitator, they should search for similar patterns in these observations.

4. Tabulate and discuss the data from all groups.

Cross-Reference Activities
1. The Conflict Cycle (Chapter 2)
2. Imaging (this chapter)
3. All activities on *Searching* (Chapter 5)
4. Self-Interest, The Fishbowl, and Compact Problem-Solving Process (Chapter 7)

Searching for Patterns of Organizational Conflict

Naming

Name or describe the conflicts that occur most often in your organization. In which of the following categories do these conflicts fall: communications, procedures, or policies?

Between Whom?

List group(s) of people who generally have conflict with one another; i.e., secretaries vs. bosses, middle managers vs. supervisors, board vs. management, union vs. management, women vs. men, minorities vs. majorities.

When Is it Happening?

Are there patterns developing as to when conflicts generally occur? If so, make a record of them.

Where Do the Conflicts Happen?

Are the conflicts public or private? Are there any places where conflicts generally emerge? Where are they resolved?

In What Phase?

Refer to the conflict cycle explained in Chapter 1 and outlined as an introductory activity in Chapter 2. In what phase is the named organizational conflict?

4

Reacting

Conflicts come in many forms. Some are overt, loud, highly charged, and complicated, while others are subtle, quiet, low-keyed, and simple. Regardless of the form of the conflict, individuals tend to react to conflicts in some set pattern. One's style of reacting to conflict is learned, along with other behaviors, attitudes, values, and beliefs. As we have explored in *Getting Started* (Chapter 2), the messages we got from adults and peers as we were growing up were established by the time we were adults. Those affective values, attitudes, and beliefs determined our future behaviors—and our styles of reacting to conflicts.

Anything learned can be relearned or reinforced, and unlearned so that new behaviors can take their place. The purpose of this chapter is to assist participants in reevaluating their individual styles of reacting to conflict. The activities encourage a look at one's dominant style of reacting to a variety of conflicts.

With this self-knowledge and awareness, participants are more likely to determine the appropriateness of behavioral patterns. The assumption behind these activities is that no one pattern of reacting is "good." Rather, we should assume that the choice of behavior, and the assessment of its effectiveness, is determined by the variables in each situation.

The activities included in this chapter explore one's style, using several methods. They include a look at how we deal with conflict in our bodies, the use of art and movement, and more cognitive analyses. In addition, one activity takes participants one more step—once a dominant style is identified, individuals are encouraged to determine the true value of that style and consider selling it at a bargain rate.

Notes to Myself

Are You Someone Who. . . ?

Objectives   To identify one's usual type of reactions to conflict

Group Size   Small groups of four to six people

Time Required   One hour

Materials Utilized   A copy for each person of the two worksheets accompanying this activity

Physical Setting   Small groups of tables and chairs

Content and Process

1. Introduce the purpose of the activity.

2. Review with the participants how styles of behaving are developed. Review the ten types of reactions.

3. Ask participants to recall several different conflicts they experienced recently. (You could refer to the Conflict Chart, if used previously.) List the conflicts on the Charting My Reactions to Conflict worksheet.

4. For each conflict listed, participants should determine which type of reaction they had, and put a check mark in the appropriate column(s) on the chart. Have them refer to the worksheet, Are You Someone Who. . .? to help them determine their type by matching their behavior and words to those on the chart. They may find that they reacted with a variety of types.

5. In small groups, participants may discuss the following questions with one another.

    a. Which types of reaction do I generally use when I face conflict?

    b. Would others who know me agree with this perception?

    c. Which of my styles of reacting were most appropriate for the conflict situation I was facing at the time? Which were inappropriate?

d. Which type would I like to increase the use of in the future?

Variations/ Comments

This activity assists awareness of one's conflict style when facing real experiences. It could be used in conjunction with other activities in this chapter (It's in the Body, Sculpting, and Feelings Collage); then contrasted with the analysis of one's reactions to hypothetical situations found in What's Your Conflict Style?

Cross-Reference Activity

Conflict Chart (Chapter 3)

Charting My Reactions to Conflicts

Recent Conflicts	Defender	Soldier	God	Diverter	Avoider	Harmonizer	Apologizer	Abdicator	Feeler	Negotiator	Observations, Comments

Are You Someone Who. . . ?

Type	Behaviors	Favorite Phrases
1. Defender	Justifies and defends position	"Let me explain." "Yes, but. . . ." "You don't understand."
2. Soldier	Fights back, threatens, punishes, seeks revenge, insults, or berates other person	"Oh, yeh?" "Says who?"
3. God	Dictates the resolution, uses power of established authority	"Of course I'm right." "Do it my way."
4. Diverter	Diverts discussion entirely or focuses on superficial issues, postpones conflict, complains to third party	"The *real* problem is. . . ." "Let's discuss this later."
5. Avoider	Avoids at all costs, ignores, doesn't become involved in situations that are conflict prone	"Let's forget it." "That doesn't bother me."
6. Harmonizer	Smooths over conflict; emphasizes harmony, peace, and warmth	"This isn't important enough to fight over. Both of us are right."
7. Apologizer	Expresses regret	"I'm sorry."
8. Abdicator	Agrees with other person, takes the blame, feels it is hopeless and gives up	"You're right. I did that wrong." "Oh well, it's hopeless to try."
9. Feeler	Expresses reaction by describing feelings	"When you . . . I feel. . . ." "I'm feeling. . . ."
10. Negotiator	Tries to find a compromise, bargains	"Let's talk this over so we can find a solution."

It's in the Body

Objectives   To identify the effects that conflict has on one's body

Group Size   Small groups of three to five people

Time Required   Two- to three-day period

Materials Utilized   A copy of the worksheet, It's in the Body

Physical Setting   Table and chairs

Content and Process

1. Introduce the activity with the statement, "Whenever there's an emotional conflict, the body has a reaction." Explain that each of us has our own style of handling conflict; thus, our bodies' reactions will also differ.

2. Ask participants to look back over earlier activities they have done which identified actual conflicts, and think about how they reacted. Have them recall the *feelings* they experienced, and where in their bodies they felt it. Using the worksheet accompanying this activity, ask them to mark the places, on the body shown, where those feelings were held or emerged during a conflict.

3. For the next two days, ask the participants to stop to determine their bodily reaction everytime they are involved in a conflict. Using the space provided below the figure, they can keep track of those bodily responses.

4. Participants should then share their observations—first in small groups of three to five people, then in a large group—asking themselves:

    a. How did each of us react to conflict in our bodies?

    b. What are some ways that these feelings are, or can be, released from our bodies?

    c. What happens to our bodies when the feelings are not released?

Variations/ Comments   Rather than collect information over a several-day period, note bodily reactions to conflicts listed on the Conflict Chart (Chapter 3).

Cross-Reference Activities   1. Conflict Chart (Chapter 3)
2. Sculpting (this chapter)

It's in the Body

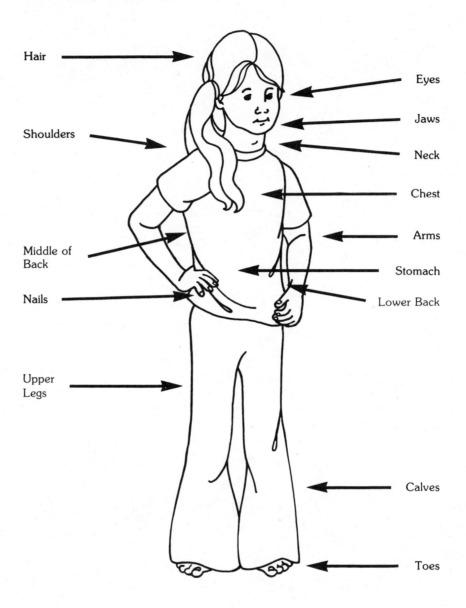

Hair

Shoulders

Middle of
Back

Nails

Upper
Legs

Eyes

Jaws

Neck

Chest

Arms

Stomach

Lower Back

Calves

Toes

Notes to Myself

Sculpting

Objectives

To identify, through body movement, how one reacts to conflicts

Group Size

Any number of pairs

Time Required

One hour

Materials Utilized

None

Physical Setting

Enough room for pairs to move freely

Content and Process

1. Prepare a series of short descriptions of conflict situations that are appropriate for the participants.

2. Ask participants to form pairs, facing one another, and identify who will be A and who will be B.

3. Read the first situation. Person A is to listen and respond to how she or he would normally react in the given situation by *sculpting* person B into a bodily position. Person B is to passively allow herself or himself to be moved into whatever position desired by A, including facial expressions. This continues until A feels B reflects the desired response.

4. Tell person A to reflect upon what he or she sees and to then talk with B about this experience. You, the trainer, should suggest questions like the following:

   a. What are you seeing? What is the message conveyed by this *sculpture?*

   b. How does it feel to see yourself in another person?

   c. How does your usual response to conflict benefit your needs and wants?

   d. How else might you respond?

5. Now, repeat the process with B listening to a new conflict situation, sculpting her or his partner, and reflecting upon the experience.

6. Additional conflict situations can be posed until both the facilitator and participant have had enough opportunity to learn more about their reaction to conflict.

Variations/ Comments

Rather than do the sculpting with hypothetical situations, participants could use real conflict examples they have experienced, such as those listed on the Conflict Chart (Chapter 3).

Cross-Reference Activities

1. Conflict Chart (Chapter 3)
2. It's in the Body (this chapter)

What Is Your Conflict Style?

Objectives
1. To identify the use of four styles of dealing with conflict
2. To identify the ways in which each style works well and does not work well
3. To get feedback from ourselves and others as to how we deal with conflict in our day-to-day relations

Materials Utilized

*Managing Conflict Awareness Profile.** A feedback instrument prepared by managers on their conflict management style.

*Managing Conflict Feedback Profile.** A feedback instrument prepared by employees (peers or co-workers) which reflects their view of how the program participant manages conflict.

*Scoring and Interpretation of the Managing Conflict Awareness Profile and the Managing Conflict Feedback Profile.** A booklet to translate scores into meaningful data.

*Managing Conflict Administrator's Guide.** A step-by-step guide to administering the instruments; a discussion guide using the race, fight, flight, or freeze conflict management model and an exercise in identifying common phrases by conflict style.

Content and Process

    1. Prepare the *Awareness* and *Feedback* profiles prior to the workshop.

    2. Present the Conflict Styles Model shown on the next page.[1]

The Conflict Styles Model presents the familiar face, fight, flight, or freeze concepts. Have participants analyze each style, in terms of their strengths and weaknesses, or in terms of their impact and ownership in a problem-solving or management situation. Both the positive and negative aspects of conflict are considered.

*© 1978, Bob Richards Consulting Associates, Inc. See source of materials.
[1]Permission granted by Bob Richards Consulting Associates, Inc.

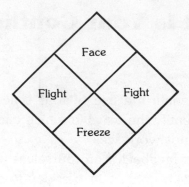

3. Conduct a concensus exercise, using the model, to ensure understanding and add feedback on the participants' communication style.

4. The participants should then score and analyze their style of dealing with conflict.

Variations/ Comments

Design of the model and the feedback instruments allow for ease of use, along with other instruments in a management seminar, to give a composite style of management.

Source of Materials

The *Managing Conflict Awareness Profile,* the *Managing Conflict Feedback Profile,* and the administrator's materials were designed by Bob Richards Consulting Associates, Inc. © 1978, revised 1980. They may be obtained from Participative Learning Materials, a division of Consulting Associates, Inc. 24133 Northwestern Highway, Suite 201, Southfield, Michigan 48075, telephone (313) 353-9510.

A complete participant package includes (1) *Managing Conflict Awareness Profile,* and (2) *Managing Conflict Feedback Profile.* The administrator's package includes (1) *Managing Conflict Administrator's Guide,* and (2) *Scoring and Interpretation of the Managing Conflict Awareness Profile and the Managing Conflict Feedback Profile* (one copy per participant).

Added feedback profiles may be desired in team building or organizational analysis as part of the operational research / data gathering effort. When used in this manner, caution must be exercised. It is recommended the author of these instruments be consulted for process consultation assistance.

Feelings Collage

Objectives To identify, through art, how one reacts to conflict

Group Size Any number

Time Required One hour

Materials Utilized Old magazines, newspapers, colored paper, scissors, glue, odds and ends, magic markers, and crayons

Physical Setting Large room or table so that materials may be spread out

Content and Process

1. Ask participants to close their eyes and recall a time when they were recently involved in a conflict. At a slow pace, present the following questions: "Who was involved? What led up to the conflict? What were your feelings? What happened? What feelings remain with you?"

2. Next, have each person create a collage or graphic representation of these feelings, with the materials supplied. Insist on quiet so that individuals can reflect without interruption.

3. Form small groups of three to five people, and ask participants to share their collage or artwork, explaining what is represented. Allow the others to ask questions that clarify the speaker's thinking, but none that challenge the speaker.

4. Reconvene everyone into a large group and have them list the range of feelings represented in their small groups.

Cross-Reference Activities

1. It's in the Body (this chapter)
2. Sculpting (this chapter)

Notes to Myself

Selling One's Style of Conflict

Objectives   To identify the consequences, positive and negative, of an individual's dominant style of dealing with conflict

Group Size   Small groups of four to five people

Time Required   Two hours

Materials Utilized   None

Physical Setting   Enough space for small groups to spread out

Content and Process   1. Before proceeding with this activity, participants should have experienced one of the earlier activities that helped them to identify their dominant style of dealing with conflicts. With that in mind, each person is to create a commercial, imagining their conflict style, or pattern, as a medical potion. They can use these questions to help them develop the commercial:

    a. What will this potion do for someone?
    b. How much potion should be taken?
    c. How often?
    d. What are its strongest selling points?
    e. What would the warning label say?
    f. What are some of the side effects of taking this potion?
    g. How would the potion be packaged?
    h. What would it sell for?
    i. Would the listed price be considered cheap or expensive for someone to buy?

2. After each person has had a chance to prepare a commercial, they can act it out or present it within their small groups. The others can then give feedback as to how they would feel about *purchasing* this style.

3. Some commercials may be presented to the whole group, so that each conflict is represented. A summary of the advantages and disadvantages of each style should be developed by the total group.

Variations/ Comments

This activity can produce a lighter atmosphere to a workshop, and yet provide the opportunity for participants to see the real value of their conflict style.

Cross-Reference Activity

What Is Your Conflict Style? (this chapter)

5

Searching

Searching for the causes of conflict is essential if we are going to be successful in resolving the present conflict and reducing the possibility of its recurrence. The search may be relatively easy, especially if the elements of the conflict are similar to past ones. However, many conflicts are complicated, long standing, and involve many variables. But, whichever type, simple or complex, the cause(s) must be sought out.

Think of a time when you might have been watching your favorite television program; a radio was on in one child's room; a cake was baking in the oven; and the washing machine and dryer were cleaning your clothes. Then, the lights flickered and several appliances stopped. What did you do? Most likely, you systematically checked out the total electrical system to find the cause of the problem. It wouldn't have taken long because you knew from past experience that the oven and dryer cannot function at the same time. However, if you hadn't had this past experience, the search may have taken longer. Assuming you found the cause (probably an overload of circuits), you were then ready to remedy the cause and resume some normalcy.

The cause of conflicts can vary greatly. This chapter offers activities that separate the various causes, realizing that this may be simplistic. However, by looking at each cause separately, participants may increase the depth of their understanding about each; and thus, enhance their own diagnostic skills when faced with future conflicts.

One cause could be when wants or needs differ. Two activities, Dialogue with Self and Want in a Hat, help participants to identify occasions when their wants or needs are in conflict with those of others. These activities also provide the chance to find out just what our, as well as others', wants or needs are.

A second cause of conflict could be when individuals' values differ. The activity, My Values, Your Values, and Our Values, looks at the types of values that can be ripe for conflicts between individuals. Values in Communication is an activity that searches for conflicts in values that are based on one's age. This instrument traces these differences to the values we each learned as we grew up in different periods of history.

A third possible cause of conflict is differing perceptions. Three activities (How Many Do You See?, Connect the Dots, and What Do You See?) explore the role that perceptions play in conflict. They demonstrate how each of us perceives even the most concrete image in different ways.

The fourth potential cause of conflict is the assumptions we draw from the information available to us. The activity, Drawing Assumptions, recognizes the role assumptions play in causing conflicts; and the activity, Testing Our Assumptions, goes the next step to check out those assumptions.

Two other areas possibly causing conflicts include when the individuals in conflict hold differing degrees of knowledge and expectations. Two activities, Do You Know What I Know? and Expectations: Mine and Theirs, facilitate how these differences have caused past conflicts.

Similar to Values in Communications is the belief that there will be conflicts between people who are different because of their gender, race, or ethnicity. Potential areas of conflict are explored in the activities, Growing Up, Growing Up Male/Female, and Growing Up White/Black. The final activity, Management of Differences, outlines a diagnostic instrument useable for searching for many causes.

Once participants understand the breadth of causes for conflicts and how several causes may relate to a particular conflict, they are more likely to apply the same systematic method of searching for causes when their own "circuits" are blown and a conflict is brewing.

Dialogue with Self

Objectives
1. To introduce the concept of subselves
2. To train participants to "listen" to their own thoughts and feelings
3. To clarify conflicting issues within self

Group Size Any number

Time Required One to two hours

Materials Utilized Extra chairs

Physical Setting Enough room for small groups to form

Content and Process

1. Tell participants you would like some volunteers. Wait a few minutes to allow some to come forward. Now ask those who volunteered to share the *sentences* that went through their minds prior to the decision to volunteer. You may help by posing the following questions: "Were there any *voices* telling you not to volunteer?" "What were they saying?" "What did the voice say which made you volunteer?" Then ask those who did not volunteer to share the sentence they said to themselves.

2. Explain that we usually have many conversations going through our heads from instant to instant throughout our lives, especially when confronted with a conflict. Our heads begin operating, with voices saying, "Do this," and "Don't do that." There are often many voices presenting several alternatives and perspectives.

3. Ask participants to tune into a conflict they are currently having in which their internal voices are carrying on a dialogue. Give them an example. Tell them to write a short dialogue or script of the conversation between the various parts of themselves.

4. Make a request for a volunteer to demonstrate her or his script. Place two chairs (or more, if more than two voices are in the script) facing each other. The volunteer is to start the dialogue in one chair, and then move to the second chair to answer himself or herself. Continue the process, switching chairs until the script is completed, or until a resolution of the conflict is found. Other group members may ask questions of either chair.

5. Hold a large group discussion about the value of sub-selves. Discuss the value of listening carefully to our inner dialogues, and explain how to use this technique to resolve internal conflicts.

Variations/ Comments

1. The whole group could be divided into small groups so that all individuals have a chance to act out their script.

2. A brief discussion of the theory of Gestalt Therapy could be presented to provide a theoretical framework for this activity.

Want in a Hat

Objectives

1. To identify some basic human wants and desires
2. To recognize the relationship between unmet wants and conflict

Group Size

Up to ten per small group

Time Required

Forty-five minutes to one hour

Materials Utilized

3" x 5" cards, and hat or empty box

Physical Setting

Circle of chairs

Content and Process

1. Give all participants an index card and ask them to do the following:

Side 1

List several wants and desires you've had this past week. List several wants and desires you've had over a longer period of time.

Side 2

Look over the list on Side 1, then complete this statement for one of the items:

"When I wanted _____,
a thought I had was _____,
and a feeling I had was _____.
However, when the want was unfulfilled, my thought was _____,
and my feeling was _____.
What I then did was to _____.

2. Collect the cards and shuffle them inside the hat or box. Ask each person to pick a card from the hat.

Permission to use this adapted activity came from Gerald Weinstein, Professor of Education, University of Massachusetts, Amherst.

3. One at a time, have each person read the new card and complete this sentence, "I imagine that this person. . . ."

4. After all of the cards have been read and responded to by the reader, the group can then discuss the conflict that occurs when wants and desires are not met. You can use these questions:

a Compare one's thoughts and feelings before and after satisfaction of a want is attempted.

b. With whom are the conflicts occurring? (With self? Others? Who?)

c. What are some ways we attempt to resolve the conflict of unmet wants and needs?

d. What are some new ways we could use to resolve the conflict of unmet wants and needs that meet the criteria of "winning resolutions?"

Variations/ Comments

A lecturette on Maslow's Hierarchy of Needs and/or W. C. Schultz's could be presented to provide a theoretical framework for understanding human behavior. Useful resources include "The Maslow Need Hierarchy," *1972 Annual Handbook for Group Facilitators* and "Human Needs and Behavior," *1975 Annual Handbook,* both from University Associates, La Jolla, California.

My Values, Your Values, and Our Values

Objectives

1. To recognize that differences between our values and those of others can be a source of conflict
2. To understand the importance of respecting one another's value positions
3. To reduce conflict by understanding and accepting one another's values

Group Size

Groups of four to six people

Time Required

One hour

Materials Utilized

My Values, Your Values, and Our Values worksheet

Physical Setting

Enough room for groups to talk privately

Content and Process

1. *Introduction*

Share the following ideas with participants to introduce the concept of values: The process of valuing is, and must be, an ongoing one in this *ever-changing* world. Clarification of our values in certain areas of our lives is needed because we tend to be confused and in conflict about them. Some of these areas include: Money, friends, family, use of time, gender, health, politics, love, sex, race, age, and so on. Once an area is clear to us, we often come into conflict with others when their values differ from ours. We can learn by looking at these areas of conflicting values.

2. *Complete chart*

The chart accompanying this activity lists several areas of conflict over values. Give each participant a copy of the chart, and instruct them as follows:

Select at least four areas; you can add your own area at the bottom.

Describe a conflict you recently had with someone else by completing the sections, Areas of Conflict and With Whom?

Next, briefly write out your own value position.

Then, try to put yourself in their shoes, writing out what you think is their value position.

3. *Resolutions*

In groups of four to five people, discuss selected areas of values. The group might like to compare experiences within the same area or randomly discuss their own areas of values conflict. The purpose of the small group discussion is to further clarify the two value positions (theirs and the other person's) and to try to determine what would be a winning resolution to the conflict. (Resolutions may be filled in on the chart.) A winning resolution would seek common ground between the two positions—a win/win solution where both positions are taken into account. Role playing can be an effective technique to assist this process.

4. *Summary*

The total group should have the opportunity to hear a summary of the value areas discussed and resolutions suggested in each of the small groups.

Variations/ Comments

This activity can be used in its entirety or only to understand another source of conflict, holding the part on resolutions until a later point.

My Values, Your Values, and Our Values

Areas of Conflict	Describe and with Whom?	Their Position	My Position	Our Winning Resolution
Money				
Friends				
Time				
Health				
Politics				
Love, Sex				
Family				
Name your own area:				

Notes to Myself

Values in Communication

Objectives

1. To identify value differences based on the events that take place during our value formation period (these differences are often referred to as the generation gap)
2. To analyze our own set of values
3. To analyze the impact of different values on day-to-day conflicts

Materials Utilized

*Values In Communication Exercise.** A participant booklet to identify and analyze different values by decades starting with the 1930s.

*Values In Communication — Administrator's Kit.** A step-by-step guide to the values exercise, complete with discussion leader's notes and overhead transparencies, group size, time required, and physical setting.

Content and Process

1. Use the *Values in Communications Exercise.* The identification of values based on events and their messages are first done individually, in teams next, and then as a group.

2. Conduct a presentation of how our values are formed, based on these ideas. The values model used in this exercise is based on the concept of developmental growth. Under this concept, our value formation period is generally between ages eight and twelve, and is based on the events and the messages we get from those events during that age period. Further, it is based on the behavioral science concepts that our behavior (what we do) is a reflection of our attitudes (what we feel), which in turn is a reflection of our values (what we think).

3. Ask each participant to analyze her or his own values.

4. Next, conduct a team exercise to help participants develop an awareness of the impact that differing values can have on conflict experienced on the job.

*© 1978, Bob Richards Consulting Associates, Inc. See source of materials.

5. Then ask each participant to identify work-related issues that reflect value differences and actions to be taken to resolve conflicts in communication.

Variations/ Comments

The exercise design works well with other communication programs, and is a useful bridge to practical application of the Morris Massey film *You Are What You Were When*. See source of materials.

Source of Materials

The *Values In Communications Exercise* and the *Values In Communication — Administrator's Kit* were designed by Bob Richards Consulting Associates, Inc. © 1978. They may be obtained from Participative Learning Materials, a division of Consulting Associates, Inc., 24133 Northwestern Highway, Suite 201, Southfield, Michigan 48075, telephone (313) 353-9510. The basic package includes twelve exercises, one administrator's guide, and a set of transparencies. Additional participant exercises can be obtained separately after the basic kit has been purchased.

The videotape *You Are What You Were When* was designed by Morris Massey, and may be obtained from Magnetic Video Corporation, 23434 Industrial Park Court, Farmington Hills, Michigan 48024.

How Many Do You See?

Objectives
1. To recognize how most concrete information can be distorted
2. To see the relationship between distortions in perceptions and sources of conflicts

Group Size   Any number

Time Required   One-half hour

Materials Utilized   Newsprint or chalkboard, drawing of Rasmussen Triangle (on worksheets or acetate), overhead projector

Physical Setting   Chairs facing front of room

Content and Process   1. Indicate that participants are going to have a little test. Ask that they do not speak to their neighbors during the test. Show them the drawing below of the Rasmussen Triangle (either on handouts, the overhead projector, or newsprint).* Ask them to count the number of triangles in the diagram. Emphasize that this is a test, and that they are to complete the task in three minutes.

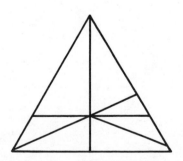

*Adapted from Rodney W. Napier and Matti K. Gershenfeld, "The Rasmussen Triangle—The Perception of Objective Facts," *Groups: Theory and Experience, Instructors Manual* (Boston: Houghton Mifflin Co., 1973), pp. 3-4.

2. On a piece of newsprint or chalkboard, write the numbers 1 to 25 in a long column. Then ask participants to raise their hands when each number is read that corresponds to the total number of triangles seen.

3. Ask for volunteers to tell or demonstrate how they came up with their particular total.

4. Discuss why the widely divergent number of responses occur, and how this distortion of concrete data could be a cause for conflict. Ask for specific examples of times in which a difference in perception was the cause of an interpersonal conflict.

Variations/ Comments
This activity can be used as an introduction before presenting the activity, Compact Problem-Solving Process (Chapter 7), to demonstrate how our perceptions can limit our ability to solve problems.

Connect the Dots

Objectives
1. To understand how our past experiences and expectations affect how we perceive phenomena
2. To see the relationship between how the rigidity and inflexibility in our perceptions affects the development and resolution of conflicts

Group Size
Any number

Time Required
One-half hour

Materials Utilized
Xerox or acetate copy of Connect the Dots worksheet, and an overhead projector

Physical Setting
Tables and chairs facing screen at front of room

Content and Process
1. Inform participants that they will be asked to solve a relatively easy problem; again, by themselves. Give each person a copy of the worksheet, which shows nine evenly spaced dots (an acetate may be used on an overhead projector). The directions include:
   a. Connect all of the dots with four straight lines
   b. Do not lift your pencil from the paper
   c. Do not retrace any line
   d. Lines may cross if necessary
2. If, after three to four minutes, participants are still struggling with the task, suggest they try solving the problem with a neighbor.

This activity was adapted from Rodney W. Napier and Matti K. Gershenfeld, "Rigidity and Inflexibility in Perception," *Groups: Theory and Experience, Instructors Manual* (Boston, Mass.: Houghton Mifflin Co., 1973), pp. 4-5.

3. Ask for volunteers to offer a solution. It is as follows:

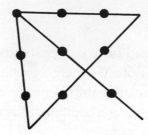

4. Discuss why so few discover the solution. Relate how the rigidity and inflexibility of our perceptions are yet another cause of conflicts between people, and how this limits our ability to seek creative solutions to conflicts.

**Variations/
Comments**

This activity can be used as an introduction to the activity, Compact Problem-Solving Process (Chapter 7), to demonstrate the necessity of moving outside the nine dots to search for alternative solutions to problems.

**Cross-Reference
Activity**

Compact Problem-Solving Process (Chapter 7)

Connect the Dots

1. Connect all of the dots with four straight lines.
2. Do not lift your pencil from the paper.
3. Do not retrace any line.
4. Lines may cross if necessary.

Notes to Myself

What Do You See?

Objectives
1. To recognize how we organize data out of an ambiguous situation, based on our past experience
2. To recognize how selective perception is a cause of interpersonal conflicts

Group Size
Groups of four to five people

Time Required
One hour

Materials Utilized
Xerox or acetate copy of W. E. Hill's drawing for PUCK.

Physical Setting
Chairs (in groups of four to five or around tables)

Content and Process
1. Present the image shown here to participants. Instruct them to privately answer the questions that follow, based on what they see.

This activity was adapted from Rodney W. Napier and Matti Gershenfeld, "The Old-Young Lady: A Classic Example," *Groups: Theory and Experience, Instructors Manual* (Boston: Houghton Mifflin Co., 1973,) pp. 7–8.

a. What is this person's age? gender? race? ethnicity?

b. From what socioeconomic class is this person?

c. What is the highest level of education this person might have had?

d. What type of occupation do you think this person has?

e. What kinds of hobbies would this person like to do?

f. On the following scale, indicate the degree to which you would trust this person:

1	2	3	4	5
Low Trust				High Trust

2. Form groups of four to five people, and have them review their observations. Request the group to reach consensus on the above question. Ask for a group report at the end of ten to fifteen minutes.

3. Discuss, in the total group, the reasons for the range of perceptions about this image, an explanation of selective perception, and how this can be another cause of interpersonal conflicts.

Variations/ Comments

Use this activity to lead into the activity, Testing Our Assumptions (this chapter), or as an introduction to the activity, Compact Problem-Solving Process (Chapter 7).

Drawing Assumptions

Objectives To recognize the role our assumptions play in causing conflicts

Group Size Small groups of six to eight people

Time Required Forty-five minutes

Materials Utilized A variety of cartoons or pictures (depicting different types of people in various social and work settings), 3″ × 5″ cards

Physical Setting Groups, seated around tables

Content and Process

1. Explain the purpose of this activity. Define the word *assumption*.

2. Hand out, or flash on an overhead projector, the first cartoon or picture. On an index card, ask all participants to describe what they *see* and any assumptions they are making about the situation depicted.

3. Each small group should discuss the responses made by its members, exploring possible effects of these assumptions.

4. Use the same process for each of the remaining cartoons or pictures. A suggested number to present is four; however, you may want to use fewer or more, depending on how quickly participants achieve the stated objectives.

5. In a large group, work with participants on a list of assumptions made about each situation, the negative effects of stereotyped assumptions, and generalizations about how our assumptions can be the cause of conflict.

6. Each person should end the activity by completing these sentences:

"I learned that I . . . ."

"I plan to . . . ."

Variations/ Comments   Make a set of envelopes, with one picture or cartoon attached to each envelope. Give one to each small group. Ask the group to write responses on an index card, put the card into the envelope, and pass the envelope to the next group. When all responses are recorded, open the envelopes, one at a time, and read the cards. Discuss.

Testing Our Assumptions

Objectives   1. To identify assumptions we make that may cause conflicts
2. To check out the accuracy of our assumptions

Group Size   Six to eight people per small group

Time Required   Two hours

Materials Utilized   A copy of the Assumption Matrix worksheet, accompanying this activity

Content and Process

1. Explain the objective of this activity, and define the word *assumption*.

2. Form participants into groups, according to their differences. Example:

Group I	Group II
Men	Women
Whites	Blacks
Managers	Employees
Old People	Young People

3. Hand out a copy of the Assumption Matrix. Separate the two groups, and have each group list the assumptions held about themselves and the other group. For example, if the two groups were divided by gender, the men would be Group I and the women would be Group II. Group I would list the assumptions they make about themselves that block their relationship with other men (box A), and those assumptions that facilitate relationships with other men (box B). They would also list assumptions they have about women that block authentic relationships with them (box C) and those that facilitate meaningful relationships with women (box D).

4. Ask the two groups to post and explain their matrix. It is important that you encourage clarifying questions only, while participants are hearing the report. They should not

argue or defend their position at this time. One group may then share examples of times when assumptions held about the other group led to conflict.

5. Hold a discussion of any currently unresolved conflicts between individuals, looking for underlying assumptions that may be causing the conflict.

6. Discuss the value of checking out assumptions.

Assumption Matrix

	Assumptions Which Block Authentic Relationships	Assumptions Which Facilitate Authentic Relationships
Assumptions Held By Group I	A	B
Assumptions Held By Group II	C	D

Notes to Myself

Do You Know What I Know?

Objectives To identify how the amount of knowledge known and unknown can be a cause of conflicts

Group Size Trios

Time Required One hour

Materials Utilized A copy of the Knowledge Matrix, accompanying this activity

Content and Process

1. Introduce the concept, *Knowledge is power.* Relate how the amount of knowledge held by individuals in a conflict can either increase the size of the conflict, or assist in its resolution.

2. Explain the Knowledge Matrix as follows:

a. *Area I: General Knowledge*
   This signifies information that both parties know. (Examples: the earth is round, or the capital of the United States is Washington, D.C.)

b. *Area II: Hoarded Knowledge*
   This is information that you know, but the other person does not know. (Examples: my greatest fear, or my grandmother's maiden name) You know the information and it is generally your choice if you want to tell another person about it.

c. *Area III: Hidden Knowledge*
   This is information that the other person knows and has chosen not to tell you. (Example: You have a mannerism, such as twisting your hair when you are nervous, and your colleagues have nicknamed you "Nervous Nelly.") This is hidden knowledge because the other person has chosen to keep it hidden from you.

d. *Area IV: Unknown Knowledge*
   This is information that is unknown to both individuals.

3. Ask individuals to recall a conflict in which they were involved recently, and identify which part of the matrix their level of knowledge was in. In trios, have them discuss how this amount of, or lack of, knowledge either alleviated or increased the conflict.

4. In the total group, discuss the following questions.

a. How do you determine how much information to reveal to others?

b. Is it harder to increase the Hidden Knowledge or the Hoarded Knowledge?

c. Why is an increase in General Knowledge desirable to avoid and resolve conflicts?

d. What are some ways we can get the information we need to know in order to resolve a conflict?

5. Allow individuals to assess a currently unresolved conflict to determine if part of the cause of the conflict might be related to the amount of information known to each person involved. Develop a plan to obtain the needed knowledge.

Variations/ Comments

This activity can lead into a fuller discussion of trust and its relationship to conflict.

Knowledge Matrix

	Known to Self	Not Known to Self
Known to Others	**I** Area of General Knowledge	**III** Hidden Knowledge
Not Known to Others	**II** Hoarded Knowledge	**IV** Unknown Knowledge

Notes to Myself

Expectations: Mine and Theirs

Objectives   1. To identify expectations we have of ourselves and those held by others
2. To clarify how conflict occurs when our expectations differ from those of others

Group Size   Any size

Time Required   One hour

Materials Utilized   A copy of the worksheet, accompanying this activity, for each person

Physical Setting   Tables or lapboards for writing

Content and Process
1. Begin by explaining how we all hold expectations for ourselves, but so do others! This is where conflicts can occur. Then present the expectations worksheet. It should be filled out as follows:
   a. Boxes: In the boxes, participants should identify the significant relationships in their lives. Here are some examples:
   Friend
   Parent
   Neighbor
   Spouse
   Child or children
   In-laws
   Boss
   Colleagues
   After labeling the boxes, have participants list two to three expectations that each of those people have for them.

The idea for this activity came from Dr. Sidney Simon, 25 Montague Road, Leveritt, Mass. 01054.

b. Circle: The center circle represents themselves. Participants are to list some expectations they have of themselves in this circle.

2. Ask them to look over all of the recorded information and do the following:

a. Draw a line with an arrow from any expectation held by another person that they accept willingly.

b. Draw a line through any expectation held by another that they reject.

3. In small groups of four to five people discuss these expectations with the following questions in mind.

a. With which person(s) are you clearest about their expectations?

b. What kinds of expectations do you willingly accept from others? Which do you reject from others?

c. What do you do when your expectations come into conflict with others?

d. What can you do differently when these expectations are in conflict?

Variations/ Comments

1. Using the same chart, ask the participants to write in two to three expectations they have for each of the persons listed.

2. Request that participants talk with each of the people on the chart to determine the accuracy of their perception of other people's expectations of them. Point out that this is an opportunity to talk with each about their expectations of them, too!

Expectations: Mine and Theirs

Name: _____

1.

2.

3.

Name: _____

1.

2.

3.

Name: _____

1.

2.

3.

Self

1.
2.
3.

Name: _____

1.

2.

3.

Name: _____

1.

2.

3.

Name: _____

1.

2.

3.

Name: _____

1.

2.

3.

Notes to Myself

Growing Up
Discovering Attitudes and Stereotypes, Based on Race and Gender

Objectives

1. To help each person become aware of attitudes and beliefs, based on race and gender that they learned while growing up
2. To show relationships between stereotyped attitudes and beliefs, and causes of conflict

Group Size

Any number of homogeneous groups of four to six people each (preferably with equal numbers of black and white groups, or male and female groups)

Time Required

Approximately two and one-half hours

Materials Utilized

A copy of the appropriate Growing Up worksheet for each participant, newsprint, and felt-tipped markers

Physical Setting

A room large enough to accommodate several subgroups comfortably, with minimal distractions; or one large room for all participants to meet together, along with smaller rooms for subgroup meetings

Content and Process

1. Decide if your objective is to search for causes of conflict based on gender *or* race. You may decide to do two searches, but it is recommended that you do one search at a time.

2. Group participants homogeneously, based on either similarity in race or gender. Groups of four to six people are preferred.

3. Explain the purpose and objectives of the activity.

4. Pass out the appropriate Growing Up worksheets to each person. Ask the participants to privately make notes on as many items as possible.

5. Ask small groups to discuss their notes and record similar responses on newsprint. For example, a men's group would list common experiences they had growing up in different stages of their lives. It should take about one hour.

6. In the total group, the homogeneous groups can share their lists. If you have more than four groups, you may have these reports done between one group of men and one of women, or one black group and one white group. In either arrangement, it is crucial for you to ensure that the information is stated as written by each group, and not challenged by the other.

7. Questions to discuss in small or total groups include:

a. To what degree was it easy to accept the accuracy of the others' experiences while growing up (male/female or white/black)?

b. Comparing our experiences in resolving conflicts while growing up, and conflicts today, what differences and similarities are there between the two groups?

c. How can the differences of experiences in growing up be another source of conflicts?

d. How can we attempt to avoid unnecessary conflicts as a result of the insights gained from this experience?

Variations/ Comments

It is important to explore other differences people have as they grow up. This activity could be adapted to look at differences based on one's religion, ethnicity, or where one grew up.

Cross-Reference Activities

1. Childhood Messages (Chapter 2)
2. Imaging (Chapter 3)

Growing Up Male/Female

Recall Your Infancy

1. What were your physical surroundings like? What colors did you see?

2. What was your life like in your family?

3. What kind of people were your mother? Father? Sisters? Brothers? Other relatives?

4. Who took care of you?

Recall Your Childhood

1. What kind of clothes did you wear?

2. Who were your friends?

3. How did your body feel to you?

4. What did you do with your friends?

5. What games/toys did you play with?

6. What was your life with your family like?

7. How did you express your feelings?

Recall Your Adolescence

1. Who were the most important people in your life?

2. What did you want to do when you got older?

3. What kind of world was this?

4. How did you express your needs and feelings?

5. How did you relate to the opposite sex?

6. How did you feel about yourself?

7. How did you resolve conflicts you had with your peers? Parents? Teachers?

As an Adult

1. How important is work to you?

2. What kind of work do you do to make money?

3. How are you treated by your colleagues? Subordinates? Boss? How do you resolve conflicts with these people?

4. How many jobs have you had?

5. What job would you like to have?

6. Do you feel that you have any value to other people?

7. Are you married?

8. What is married life like? How do you resolve conflicts with your spouse?

9. Do you have any children? How do you resolve conflicts with your children?

10. What kind of life do you think your children will have?

11. What will their futures be like?

12. Are you getting everything you want in your life?

13. What do you do to get what you want?

14. What kinds of satisfactions have you had?

15. Does anyone know who you really are?

16. With whom do you share leisure time activities?

17. What kinds of disappointments or difficulties have you had?

18. Do you feel that anyone really cares what happens to you?

Growing Up White/Black

Recall Your Infancy

1. What were your physical surroundings like?

2. What was your life like in your family?

3. What kind of people were your mother? Father? Sisters? Brothers? Other relatives?

4. Who took care of you?

Recall Your Childhood

1. What kind of clothes did you wear?

2. Who were your friends?

3. How did your body feel to you?

4. What did you do with your friends?

5. What was your life with your family like?

Recall Your Adolescence

1. Who were the most important people in your neighborhood?

2. What did you want to do when you got older?

3. What was your neighborhood community like? Did you like the way it looked? Smelled?

4. How did you want to live?

5. What kind of world was this?

6. How long did you go to school? Why did you leave? How old were you when you left?

7. Did you ever meet a black (white) person?

8. What did you think about black (white) people?

9. How did you resolve conflicts you had with your peers? Parents? Teachers?

As an Adult

1. What kind of work do you do to make money?

2. How many jobs have you had?

3. How do you resolve conflicts you have on the job?

4. Do you feel that you have any value to other people?

5. Are you married?

6. What is your married life like? How do you resolve conflicts with your spouse?

7. Do you have any children? How do you resolve conflicts with your children?

8. What kind of life do you think your children will have?

9. What will their futures be like?

10. Are you getting everything you want in your life?

11. What do you do in your neighborhood?

12. What do you do to get what you want?

13. What kinds of satisfactions have you had?

14. Does anyone know who you really are?

15. What kinds of disappointments or difficulties have you had?

16. Do you feel that anyone really cares what happens to you?

Management of Differences

Objectives	1. To diagnose the causes and underlying factors 2. To recognize stages of evolution of conflicts
Group Size	Initially, any number; in the second part, groups of three
Time Required	One to three hours
Materials Utilized	Management of Differences instrument (see source of materials)
Content and Process	Jacqueline Rumley has drawn upon an article written by Warren Schmidt and Robert Tannenbaum, "Management of Differences," *Harvard Business Review* (November/December 1960) to develop this instrument. Part I raises important diagnostic questions for determining the nature of a conflict, including facts, goals, methods, and values. It also lists five stages of evolution of the conflict and asks participants to identify the stage in which their conflict is. Part II requires groups of three to concentrate on the nature, underlying factors, and stages as they collaboratively seek alternative solutions.
Source of Materials	The Management of Differences instrument is copyrighted, but it can be purchased through Development Publications, 5605 Lamar Road, Washington, D.C. 20016, telephone (301) 320-4409.

Notes to Myself

6

Preventing

A re there some conflicts that should or could be avoided? What methods could be used to lessen the ballooning effect of some conflicts?

This chapter provides the opportunity for participants to look at preventing some unnecessary conflicts. It is assumed that the close monitoring of factors in an organization and in a relationship can prevent the development of future conflicts. Thus, participants can apply the information learned in Chapter 5, *Searching,* on the various causes of conflict to diagnose their current situations. The activity titled, Avoiding Conflicts When You Can, lists many methods to prevent the development of conflicts.

The second assumption made is that uncovering suppressed wants and needs frequently and early enough can help prevent the ballooning of conflicts that make it more difficult to resolve. Two separate activities address this problem of suppression, called *gunnysacking.*

Notes to Myself

Checking on the Climate

Objectives   To identify potential areas of conflict through an assessment of the climate of a group or organization

Group Size   Up to twenty-five per session

Time Required   Two to four hours

Materials Utilized   A copy of the worksheet, Checking on the Climate

Physical Setting   Tables and chairs

Content and Process

1. This activity can be used to diagnose the climate or atmosphere of a small group, unit or subsystem, or to look at a total system or organization. It is important to focus on only one system or subsystem at a time.

2. Give the objectives of the activity and the procedure to be used to the members of the selected system to be diagnosed.

3. Explain each part of the worksheet.

a. Explain that the metaphor of organizational weather is the basis of the assessment. Have participants think of the various factors determining actual climate. Relate these factors to an organization.

b. *Total amount of energy:* There are internal factors that contribute to climate. Examples include overstaff systems, young vs. old. External factors include competition from other organizations, and the nature of our society and marketplace. Parts or subsystems of an organization may demonstrate differing levels of energy. The worksheet lists several factors contributing to both low and high energy.

c. *Distribution of energy within organizations:* The climate can be assessed by looking at the available energy and how it is distributed within the organization. There are several factors listed in the worksheet that look at this distribution. As each is considered (such as how much energy is expended within the organization just to keep things running) participants should determine to what degree that generally happens. If it happens quite often, they mark "high"; if occasionally, mark "moderate"; or if infrequently, mark "low."

d. *Growth:* This section looks at the extent to which the organization is good for the growth of the people working there. Growth means the development of new skills, abilities, and capacities that is beyond what is already known. The worksheet identifies many factors that can both positively and negatively affect individuals' growth. Instruct the participants to mark the appropriate column.

e. *Pleasure:* To what degree do people like working in this organization? Many of the factors listed in the other sections can help participants to assess their pleasure. Included in this section is a question on the degree of security participants feel.

f. *Describe your organization's climate:* Tell participants to summarize their assessments in this section by describing the organization's atmosphere as either "hot," "lukewarm," or "cold."

4. Request participants to individually assess the climate of their organization, making additional notes where helpful.

5. Form small groups, either homogeneously by interest or roles in the system, or heterogeneously. These small groups then compare their assessments and try to reach consensus on their perceptions. The purpose is to collect general information on the organization's climate with a few examples for each category. Thirty minutes to one hour should be sufficient.

6. In the total group, each small group reports on their assessments. Write the key ideas and potential areas of conflict on a chalkboard or newsprint.

7. Participants should then decide what will be done with these identified areas of potential conflict. The decision makers may decide to formulate new policies or procedures; task forces may be formed; or the total group might rank the most important areas and use resolving techniques such as problem solving found in Chapter 7, called *Resolving*.

Variations/ Comments

1. The facilitator might develop a special climate assessment instrument that includes factors that are especially pertinent to the system under study.

2. The assessment data could be gathered prior to the workshop.

3. The group could summarize climate factors in the Forced Field analysis format. (See Forces for and against Resolution in Chapter 7.)

4. Since the climate of a system changes as factors change, this assessment might be done periodically to identify new areas of potential conflict.

Suggested Resource

A useful book for understanding an organization's climate is Fritz Steele and Stephen Jenks, *The Feel of the Workplace* (Reading, Mass.: Addison-Wesley), 1977.

Checking on the Climate

Total Energy Available in an Organization   Consider each of these factors and determine how each contributes to high vs. low energy expended in the organization.

Factors	Examples	Results in Low Energy	Results in High Energy
1. Group Norms	For or against producing work.		
2. Management Style	Laissez-faire vs. tightly controlled		
3. Competition	Within organization Within marketplace		
4. Stability	Stable vs. rapidly growing organization		
5. Atmosphere	Presence of tension or conflict		

Distribution of Energy within an Organization   Consider each of these factors and determine to what degree—high, moderate, or low—each exists in your organization.

What Amount Is:	High	Moderate	Low
1. Used to keep things running (for example, reporting, memos, meetings, paperwork, etc.)			
2. Given as rewards for work done			
3. Expended for long-term goal-oriented activities vs. short-term or survival-oriented activities			
4. Available in resources to help people get their jobs done			
5. Is diverted into energy to resolve new crisis or develop new projects			
6. Used for infighting between subsystems			

Growth   Determine to what degree each of the following factors exist in your organization that affect individuals' development of new skills, abilities, and capacities.

To What Degree:	High	Moderate	Low
1. Does the group or organization provide opportunities for personal long-term growth and development?			
2. Are exploration, "stretching," and experimentation encouraged?			
3. Are others tolerant of different learning styles?			
4. Is the group flexible to changing needs?			
5. Do individuals help decide the roles they'll play?			

Pleasure   Assess how you feel about being in this organization by considering these questions. List some examples to support your assessment.

To What Degree:	High	Moderate	Low
1. Do people like being in this group or organization?			
2. Do people feel secure or safe?			

Describe your organization's climate   Which of these best describe the atmosphere in your organization?

Hot   Lukewarm   Cold

|—————————————|—————————————|

Notes to Myself

Gunnysacking: The Garbage Pail

Objectives

1. To make participants aware of the number of conflicts that go unresolved
2. To provide a means for the disposal of relatively unimportant conflicts
3. To prevent the escalation of conflict

Group Size   Any number

Time Required   The activity requires several days to one week

Materials Utilized   One box, envelope, or can per person

Physical Setting   Tables and chairs

Content and Process

1. Discuss with participants the objective of this activity: to help identify the number of conflicts that arise and go unresolved over a short period of time.

2. Give each person a box, small can, or envelope, and ask them to decorate or label it in a way that it will be identified as their own. The item will be the Garbage Pail—the receptacle for unresolved conflicts.

3. Over a period of time (to be determined by you or the participants) each unresolved conflict that arises is described on slips of paper by the participants and put in the Garbage Pail.

4. At the end of the collection period, ask all persons to dump out their pile and sort them according to:
   a. Those conflicts that could be easily discarded
   b. Those that need minimal attention to resolve
   c. Those requiring more effort to resolve.

5. Those in a pile "a," easily discarded, are publicly disposed of in a large garbage pail or trash can. Ask the participants to say what they are ridding themselves of as they throw the conflicts away in the can.

6. Give the participants a chance to discuss how they feel (either in small groups or in the total group) about disposing of these particular conflicts. Help them recognize conflicts that should be given away, disposed of and forgotten, rather than hung onto. They can also set personal goals for the kinds of conflicts that they will more quickly "dump" when they emerge in the future.

7. Deal with the remaining conflicts found in piles "b" and "c" by using activities found in Chapter 7, *Resolving*.

Variations/ Comments

1. You may not want to make the dramatic point of actually "dumping" conflicts, but rather have participants gather unresolved conflicts, sort them, and then move on to methods of resolving them.

2. Participants may want to identify those unresolved conflicts that they would like to "dump" or pass onto someone else.

Cross-Reference Activity

Gunnysacking: Sock Day (this chapter)

Gunnysacking: Sock Day

Objectives
1. To make participants aware of their tendency to suppress conflict
2. To provide a vehicle to express feelings around suppressed conflict
3. To prevent the escalation of conflict

Group Size   Any number

Time Required   Ten to fifteen minutes

Materials Utilized   One stuffed sock per person

Physical Setting   A room private enough to allow for excessive noise

Content and Process

1. Ask participants to identify any number of conflicts that have been suppressed, gone underground, or gunnysacked by them during the past week. They could use information gathered in activities found in Chapter 3, *Naming,* or Chapter 4, *Reacting.*

2. Give each person an old, clean sock filled with soft materials, paper, cloth, or other old socks.

3. Place the participants in two lines, about five or six feet apart, facing each other.

Row One: X   X   X   X   X
Row Two: X   X   X   X   X

4. Tell each person to recall a suppressed conflict and the feelings they still have about it. They are to imagine that the person(s) involved in the unresolved conflict is standing across from them. At your signal, everyone should simultaneously wave their sock, swinging it at the person across from them, yelling and shouting as much as they like.

5. Continue this for only a few minutes.

6. Ask each person to reflect on how he or she now feels.

**Variations/
Comments**

1. Other activities found in Chapter 7, *Resolving,* may be used, such as Compact Problem-Solving Process or Act it Out to help participants look at alternative methods to resolve conflict situations.

2. This activity could be done on a regular basis. If participants know they will have a chance to ventilate their feelings around unresolved conflicts, they will look forward to this routine, though brief, activity.

Reducing Defensive Behavior

Objectives

1. To identify key elements that contribute to defensiveness
2. To reduce the growth of conflict by changing factors causing defensive behavior

Group Size

Dyads

Time Required

One hour

Materials Utilized

Chalkboard or newsprint

Content and Process

1. Introduce the objectives of the activity.

2. Form dyads. Ask participants to think of a time when they were having a conflict with someone else and felt defensive. Together, try to determine what it was about that situation and the behaviors of those involved that caused this defensiveness. Tell participants to make a list.

3. Present the following information on the five conditions that generally produce defensiveness climate:

   a. Individuals *evaluate* what is said and done rather than *describe* what is happening.

   b. The purpose is to *control* others and the situation rather than collaborating on resolving the conflict.

   c. There is a *strategy* operating rather than a free-flowing, spontaneous movement.

   d. An attitude of *indifference* or *neutrality* exists rather than *empathy*.

   e. A *superior* rather than *equal* relationship exists.

4. In dyads, apply this information to the situations being discussed. Ask participants to determine how the existing conditions and behaviors could have been modified, in oneself and in the other person, so that the size of the conflict would have been reduced.

Cross-Reference Activity

Conflict Chart (Chapter 3) could be assessed for defensive reactions.

Notes to Myself

Avoiding Conflicts
When You Can

Objectives
1. To identify those conflicts that could be easily reduced
2. To identify methods to reduce the ballooning of unnecessary conflicts

Group Size   Twenty-five

Time Required   Forty-five minutes to one hour

Materials Utilized   Newsprint or chalkboard

Content and Process

1. Ask the question, "In what situations is it appropriate to avoid some conflicts?" List the ideas on newsprint or the chalkboard.

2. Review the diagnosis tool of locating causes of conflicts (as fully outlined in Chapter 5, *Searching*). Participants should then create a list of methods that could be used to reduce unnecessary conflicts and to reduce the ballooning of unnecessary conflicts. Their lists might include:

a. Be honest with oneself. (See Dialogue with Self (Chapter 5).)

b. Recognize and accept differences in values, perceptions, expectations, gender, race. (See Chapter 5, *Searching*.)

c. Redefine expectations and roles on a regular basis (See Expectations: Mine and Theirs (Chapter 5).)

d. Take time to get to know others with whom you interact frequently so you really know their beliefs, values, and attitudes (See My Values, Your Values, and Our Values (Chapter 5).)

e. Don't automatically assume you are right and they are wrong. Check out assumptions. (See Testing Our Assumptions (Chapter 5).)

f. Review the structures and decision-making methods being used. Modify any that would enhance better relations.

g. Review the organization's "climate." (See Checking on the Climate (this chapter).)

h. Assess the uses of power; select positive types.

i. Don't feel rejected personally if others disagree with your ideas.

j. Learn and practice attentive listening skills. (See Chapter 7, *Resolving*.)

k. Provide a method for individuals to ventilate their pent-up feelings (See Gunnysacking (this chapter).)

l. Commit yourselves to seeing that everyone will participate in reviewing what was learned from *each* conflict and apply this to any future conflicts.

Cross-Reference Activities

To identify those conflicts that could be avoided, see

1. Gunnysacking: The Garbage Pail (this chapter)
2. Conflict Scale (Chapter 7)

7

Resolving

Basic to the success of resolving conflicts were earlier efforts to accurately and thoroughly name the conflict and identify its causes. This chapter's activities assume that the training design has included this essential preparation for successful resolution of conflict.

The activities in *Resolving* fall into four categories. The first includes two activities that help participants assess readiness to deal with a conflict. The Self-Interest activity looks at the consequential benefits for the parties to resolve the conflict, while the activity Forces for and against Resolution lists those variables that help and hinder successful resolution. These two activities are crucial to participants because they clarify the attitudes that are needed for conflict resolution. A positive attitude can hasten the resolution process and leave both parties with good feelings about each other.

The second category includes two activities that investigate the key issues to be resolved. The Conflict Scale activity is a simple method to determine the degree of seriousness of a conflict between two people. The activity of Ranking and Negotiating Conflict Issues ranks the key issues into their order of importance.

The third and fourth categories look at how we can resolve conflicts. The third one focuses on procedures the participants can use, including setting rules (Fighting Fairly), learning and applying skills of listening and counseling (Tell Me and I'll Listen, and The Counselor), and utilizing role playing (Act it Out and Round Robin: Rotating Chairs).

The fourth category of conflict resolution activities uses the five basic methods outlined on the accompanying chart. The five methods include (1) denial or withdrawal, (2) suppression or smoothing over, (3) power or dominance, (4) compromise or negotiation, and (5) collaboration. The chart lists what is involved when each method is used and gives situations in which it is both appropriate and inappropriate to use each method. The assumption made here is that the appropriateness of the selected method is not what style or philosophy a person has, but rather what the situation dictates is needed. This material can be used as an introduction to any activities on resolving conflict, but is basic to the case studies found in the Five Methods of Resolving Conflicts activity.

The skills of negotiation or compromise are learned and practiced in two activities (The Fishbowl and Ranking and Negotiating Conflict Issues). The Compact Problem-Solving Process activity utilizes the collaborative conflict resolution method.

Five Basic Methods for Resolving Conflict

Methods	What Happens When Used:	Appropriate to Use When:	Inappropriate to Use When:
Denial or Withdrawal	Person tries to solve problem by denying its existence. Results in win/lose.	Issue is relatively unimportant; timing is wrong; cooling off period is needed; short-term use.	Issue is important; when issue will not disappear, but build.
Suppression or Smoothing Over	Differences are played down; surface harmony exists. Results in win/lose in forms of resentment, defensiveness, and possible sabotage if issue remains suppressed.	Same as above, also when preservation of relationship is more important at the moment.	Reluctance to deal with conflict leads to evasion of an important issue; when others are ready and willing to deal with issue.
Power or Dominance	One's authority, position, majority rule, or a persuasive minority settles the conflict. Results in win/lose if the dominated party sees no hope for self.	When power comes with position of authority; when this method has been agreed upon.	Losers have no way to express needs; could result in future disruptions.
Compromise or Negotiation	Each party gives up something in order to meet midway. Results in win/lose if "middle of the road" position ignores the real diversity of the issue.	Both parties have enough leeway to give; resources are limited; when win/lose stance is undesirable.	Original inflated position is unrealistic; solution is watered down to be effective; commitment is doubted by parties involved.
Collaboration	Abilities, values, and expertise of all are recognized; each person's position is clear, but emphasis is on group solution. Results in win/win for all.	Time is available to complete the process; parties are committed and trained in use of process.	The conditions of time, abilities, and commitment are not present.

Notes to Myself

Self-Interest

Objectives	1. To identify individual and organizational self-interest in resolving a conflict
	2. To commit self (or organization) to resolving a conflict
Group Size	Any size
Time Required	Forty-five minutes to one hour
Materials Utilized	Worksheets: What's in it for Me? and What's in it for the Organization to Resolve the Conflict?
Physical Setting	Tables and chairs
Content and Process	1. Introduce the participants to the concept of self-interest. It is graphically shown here as a group of individuals, separate from one another. Discuss how all of us, whether personally or organizationally, commit ourselves to change based on our own self-interest. We cannot move toward resolution until we know how it will personally benefit us.

2. Ask participants to focus on either a personal or an organizational conflict. Request that they complete the accompanying exercise, listing a conflict and then identifying what's in it for them to find a solution.

3. Discuss observations in either small or large group

4. Make a decision as to which resolution methods will be used.

Variations/ Comments Participants can also explore their self-interest in the other area (personal/organizational).

What's in it for Me?

The Problem   Briefly write out the conflict you are having with someone else:

Forms of Self-Interest   Which of these would meet your needs? Why bother? Explain.

_____ I would avoid getting punished, reprimanded, fired, scolded, or criticized if I resolved this conflict.

_____ I would receive some form of reward, promotion, or opportunity to grow.

_____ I would be admired by my peers, parents, boss, friend, or spouse.

_____ I would be a good, loyal citizen or member of my organization.

_____ I would successfully demonstrate my ability to work with those with whom I differ or who hold different views or values than I.

_____ I would be truly authentic—true to myself and true to others.

The Goal   To move from separate self-interests to common self-interests

What's in it for the Organization to Resolve the Conflict

The Problem   Briefly write out the conflict that the organization is facing:

Forms of Self-Interest   How would the organization benefit if this conflict were resolved? Explain.

_____   It would avoid bad publicity, class action suits, sabotage, strikes, loss in productivity or production, or low test scores.

_____   It would have a more satisfied work force with better delivery of service, higher production, or higher test scores.

_____   It would be viewed as an exemplary model to another organization, or to the community.

_____   It would be consistently acting on stated organizational policy.

_____   It would increase its standing in the profession, industry, or community; its reputation would attract others to work with it or want to be involved in it in the future.

_____   It would be a truly authentic organization—true to its goals and true to society.

The Goal   To move from separate forms of self-interest to a larger, common one

Notes to Myself

Forces for and against Resolution

Objective To identify variables that can help and hinder the successful resolution of a conflict

Group Size Twenty to twenty-five people

Time Required Thirty minutes

Materials Utilized Newsprint or chalkboard

Physical Setting Chairs facing front of room

Content and Process

1. Explain the objective of this activity to the participants.
2. Define the key conflict and review the possible causes. Next, identify the desired outcome.
3. Draw this diagram on the newsprint or chalkboard:

4. Together, list as many variables or forces that might help facilitate the successful resolution of the problem and those that would work against its resolution. Examples might include time, attitudes of people involved, complexity of the issue, skills of those involved in the conflict, and history of the conflict.
5. Remind participants that the goal is to reduce or eliminate the restraining forces. Ask the group to think of ways in which to do this and to develop any necessary plans to make this happen.

Cross-Reference Activity Conflict Scale (this chapter)

Notes to Myself

Conflict Scale

Objective   To determine the degree of seriousness of a conflict

Group Size   Any size

Time Required   Ten to fifteen minutes

Materials Utilized   Chalkboard or newsprint

Physical Setting   Any arrangement would work

Content and Process

1. When an issue emerges and you want to quickly measure how serious the conflict is, ask those in the dispute to rate their sentiments on the following scale:

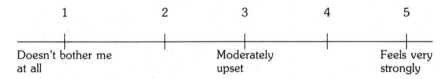

1	2	3	4	5
Doesn't bother me at all		Moderately upset		Feels very strongly

2. If one party feels at least two points stronger than the other, then it is agreed that the person with the lower value concedes in favor of the person with the more intense feelings.

3. If both parties feel strongly about the issue, then they recognize the conflict needs attention and time. They next agree on the resolution technique to be used.

Cross-Reference Activities

1. The Counselor (this chapter)
2. Tell Me and I'll Listen (this chapter)
3. Compact Problem-Solving Process (this chapter)

Notes to Myself

Ranking and Negotiating Conflict Issues

Objectives
1. To identify key conflict issues and rank order them
2. To negotiate the issues in the order of importance

Group Size
Two groups (five to ten in each) who are in conflict with one another

Time Required
Thirty minutes to one hour for ranking issues (the time necessary to negotiate would depend upon the number and complexity of the conflict issues)

Materials Utilized
Pre-printed Conflict Issue cards.

Physical Setting
Large table for two groups to face one another, and separate rooms for two groups to meet privately.

Content and Process

1. Review the objectives of the activity with the participants.

2. The two groups in conflict with one another meet separately. Tell both groups to complete one Conflict Issue card per issue important to them. The card looks like this:

The Conflict Issue is _____
_____ .

It is important because _____
_____ .

Aspects we'd be willing to negotiate include: _____
_____ .

---

3. Sort the cards into their order of importance to all the group members.

4. The two groups meet at a large table facing each other. One spokesperson from each group presents the key issues in order of importance. You should then look for

those issues that both groups agree are of lowest importance and of highest importance. Attempt to reach total group agreement on the rank order of issues to be negotiated.

5. Lead the discussion of the issue of lowest importance first, then move to each issue in increasing order of importance until all are resolved.

Variations/ Comments

This activity works well with an intergroup conflict vs. the Conflict Scale worksheet (this chapter) that helps to sort out issues on an interpersonal level.

Cross-Reference Activities

1. The Fishbowl (this chapter)
2. Compact Problem-Solving Process (this chapter)

Fighting Fairly

Objective To develop a list of ground rules that ensures a fair process for both persons involved in a conflict

Group Size Any number—regrouped into trios and later into groups of six

Time Required Two hours

Materials Utilized Newsprint or chalkboard

Physical Setting Enough space so small groups can work privately

Content and Process

1. Clarify the purpose for this activity to the participants. Ensure that the problem between the individuals is fixed or resolved, not that blame is placed, nor that anyone is threatened, humiliated, or overwhelmed.

2. Ask the participants to reflect upon a time they had a conflict with someone who did not "fight fairly." Separate the participants into groups of three, and ask the trios to share their thoughts. Next, ask the trios to recall and share a time when *they* did not "fight fairly." This sets the stage for identifying what conditions and behaviors are not desirable when conflict is inevitable and a resolution is sought.

3. Next, ask the participants to fantasize the ideal conditions and behaviors that would be found in a situation in which fighting would be done fairly. Each trio should make a list and share it with the total group. The list of items may be presented on newsprint or the chalkboard.

4. Form groups of six and ask these groups to create a list of ground rules that could be used when interpersonal conflict occurs.

5. After about twenty minutes, ask each group to present its report. The ground rules should then be grouped, synthesized, and rewritten until the total group reaches con-

sensus on the list. (You may want to list some suggested ground rules to serve as a guide.)

6. Give each person a copy of the ground rules.

Variations/ Comments   The group may decide to use the ground rules whenever conflict occurs among its members.

Cross-Reference Activity   The Counselor (this chapter)

Suggested Resource   In-depth understanding of how to resolve fights can be found in George R. Bach and Peter Wydess, *The Intimate Enemy: How to Fight Fair in Love and Marriage* (New York: Avon Books, 1970).

Fighting Fairly—Some Ground Rules

Purpose The parties in the conflict agree that the goal is to fix the problem—not assign blame, hurt, humiliate, or threaten.

Timing Both parties agree as to when they will work out the solution. (Timing means individual readiness, psychologically, physically, and mentally, to invest energy in resolving the conflict.)

Commitment Both parties agree to stick it out until an equitable solution is found—neither party will avoid the issue or run away from it.

Mediator Both parties participate in the decision as to whether or not a third party or mediator is needed. If one is desired, both parties must agree as to who that person will be—preferably someone who is objective to the problem, flexible, assertive about moving things along, has a sense of humor, and has the ability to cut through the superficialities to the meat of the problem.

Place A place that is comfortable and neutral is best. It should provide privacy and be free of all kinds of interruptions.

Food and Drink No drugs or alcohol will be consumed. Refreshments and food should be available as needed.

Recording Both parties need to agree on how the issues and resolutions will be recorded: newsprint, tape recorder, third party, etc.

Confidentiality Both parties agree that whatever happens in the conflict session will remain confidential. Only the terms of any agreement are made public and are published jointly.

Bad-Mouthing The parties agree not to bad-mouth each other before or after the session.

Other Supporters Both parties have the right to invite one other person to attend the session. These supporters lend aid and comfort to each person, can provide useful information (only when asked by the mediator), and generally are available to lend emotional support in a trying situation.

Notes to Myself

Tell Me and I'll Listen

Objective To learn and apply a three-step process of initiating and resolving a conflict issue

Group Size Any number; trios are used after the demonstration

Time Required Two hours

Materials Utilized Newsprint or chalkboard

Physical Setting Chairs facing front of the room or in a circle

Content and Process

1. Ask a volunteer to come forward to talk about a conflict she or he currently has with someone else in the group. Both parties must grant permission to participate. Person *E* is the one expressing a complaint, while person *H* is the one hearing it.

2. Explain the following process to the participants before it is applied:

Step One

Person *E* completes one of these statements:

I feel . . .

I do not like it when . . .

I am upset . . .

I am irritated . . .

I am annoyed . . .

Step Two

Person *E* next completes one of these statements:

I want you to . . .

I demand that you . . .

I wish you would . . .

Step Three

Person *E* finally completes one of these statements:

I appreciate your position . . .

I imagine that you feel . . .

Person *E* is guided through each of these three steps while person *H* listens.

3. Explain the second part of the process to the participants before it is applied:

Step One

Person *H* completes one of these statements:

I heard you saying . . .

I see you . . .

Step Two

Person *H* next projects what he or she thinks is behind the statements made earlier by *E* by completing this statement:

I imagine that you . . .

Step Three

Person *H* proposes what he or she is willing to do by completing one of these statements:

I can . . .

I will . . .

I plan to . . .

I will try to . . .

Person *H* is guided through each of these steps while person *E* listens.

4. Ask person *E* to further clarify, expand, or react to what person *H* has presented, using some of the incomplete sentences so that "I . . ." statements and not "You . . ." statements are made by the person with the complaint. Alternate this process with responses from person *H* who is also asked to continue using the incomplete sentences designated for person *H*.

5. Continue these steps until both parties are satisfied.

6. Next, ask the rest of the participants to form trios. If individuals have conflicts with others in the room, these should be paired up, along with a third neutral party. If, however, some participants want to work on current conflicts with others not present, they can do so by asking the

two others in the trio to role-play the part of the *H* person. Give each member of the trio an opportunity to be person *E,* presenting a conflict to the other two who act as person *H.*

Cross-Reference Activity   The Counselor (this chapter)

Notes to Myself

The Counselor

Objective
To introduce the role of a counselor or mediator in an interpersonal conflict

Group Size
Any size

Time Required
One to two hours

Materials Utilized
None

Physical Setting
Chairs facing front of room or in a circle

Content and Process
1. Discuss with the participants how on some occasions the presence of a third party can help in resolving a conflict. Examples may include:
   When couples continually rehash and do not resolve issues
   When the emotional level of the conflict escalates to a dangerous or irrational point
   When co-workers or students just don't get along
   When continual friction or hostility interferes with getting a job done.

2. Explain the criteria of an effective counselor or mediator. You may want to refer to those listed in the activity on ground rules, Fighting Fairly (in this chapter).

3. Demonstrate how a counselor can assist two parties in conflict. Ask for two volunteers to present a problem between them. Ask one to start by explaining what the problem is, to express her or his feelings fully, and to state what changes are desired in the second person. (This process is similar to the three steps in the Tell Me and I'll Listen exercise, except the counselor leads the discussion and can work on more complex conflicts with the parties.) You now act as the counselor, and ask the second person to also clarify

what she or he perceives as the problem, to express feelings, and to state desired outcomes. Continue this process of expression, listening, paraphrasing, further clarification, and negotiation until a solution or agreement is found that is satisfactory to both parties.

4. Ask other participants to volunteer to present a current conflict they are having. Form small groups around these people. Tell two of the group members to act as counselors, applying the steps and appropriate behaviors as discussed and demonstrated. If there are still extra participants, they may be observers.

Variations/ Comments

You may act as the counselor for each participant wishing to present a conflict.

Cross-Reference Activities

1. Fighting Fairly (this chapter)
2. Tell Me and I'll Listen (this chapter)

Act it Out

Objectives
1. To teach the steps of role-playing
2. To use role-playing as means to clarify the conflict and find a solution

Group Size   Any size for demonstration

Time Required   One hour

Materials Utilized   Tables, chairs, and other props as needed

Physical Setting   Enough space for roles to be acted out

Content and Process

1. Explain to the participants how role-playing can help in finding solutions to conflicts. Since the process of role-playing may be unfamiliar to participants, the first example is done with the whole group.

2. Select a problem, either one that the whole group has been wrestling with, or perhaps one suggested by a participant, or a hypothetical one.

3. Clarify details about the problem by asking the participants the following questions:
   a. What is the conflict?
   b. What is behind the problem?
   c. Who are the chief characters? How does each feel? What does each want?
   d. What other characters are involved in the conflict?

4. Set the stage for the role-play. Ask for volunteers to play the role of each of the main characters. Determine the scene:
   a. Where is it happening?
   b. What props are needed?
   c. How will the action start?

Prepare the audience by asking them to observe different characters' behaviors.

5. Start the role-play. Generally, the most effective role-play is brief. Because it never reaches a climax and conclusion, you should cut the action at the earliest moment when you think that enough data has been produced for analysis and discussion.

6. Freeze the action. Stop the role-play and ask the audience, "What do you think the character should do now?" Additional side coaching can be done by asking the characters how they are feeling, or what else they might try to do.

7. Resume the role-play until you once again determine that the action should be stopped.

8. Guide the role-play toward a solution. Perhaps set a time limit on the solution-seeking period.

9. Hold a discussion of the problem that was role-played by asking the following questions:

   a. What were the sources of the conflict as revealed by the characters?

   b. What attitudes were revealed by the behaviors of the actors?

   c. Did anything happen that really couldn't have happened?

   d. What were the feelings of the characters at certain points?

   e. Which of the solutions do you think would work best? Who would it benefit? Who will be unhappy?

   f. What additional solutions could be tried for this problem?

Variations/Comments

1. Once participants understand the process of role-playing, they can form small groups to act out additional problems.

2. Additional roles that can be used in role-playing include:

   a. *Doubling*

   You, as the facilitator, may act as a double or you may use a participant. The double copies the posture and facial expressions of the role-player. This gives the role-player feedback about his or her interpretation of the role. Doubling gives more people a chance to get in touch with each role. The double should stand or sit as close to the role-player as possible. Prepare the double by telling him or her to feel what the role-player feels. For example, "He's tense, nervous, happy, etc."

b. *Alter Ego—An Extension of the Double*
The alter-ego stands or sits in back of the role-player. It is not necessary to copy posture or facial expressions. The alter-ego *speaks the innermost thoughts* of the role-player. For example, another character really puts down the role-player, who decides to respond politely. In the role-player's mind, he or she is calling the other character names or thinking things that aren't so polite. (To assist the alter-ego, you may want to coach: "What *isn't* the role-player saying? What does the role-player *really* want to say?" etc.) The alter-ego picks up these thoughts and speaks them for the role-player. When speaking these thoughts, *the alter-ego speaks as the role-player.* The alter-ego and the role-player *become one.* The alter-ego makes the thoughts of the role-player explicate. This gives depth to the role-play and dimension to the role.

3. Have the main characters reverse their roles part way through the role-play. This allows the person who has the conflict to experience the other character's position.

4. Role-play the parts by having the players sit back-to-back so that the on-lookers can see both, but the players must rely on their voices to communicate. This will help them to see the difference between communicating with and without the aid of body language.

Cross-Reference Activities

1. Act it Out (this chapter)
2. Round Robin: Rotating Chairs (this chapter)
3. Compact Problem-Solving Process (this chapter)

Notes to Myself

Round Robin: Rotating Chairs

Objective   To apply one's knowledge of resolution techniques to a variety of conflict situations

Group Size   Groups of twelve

Time Required   One hour minimum

Materials Utilized   Sets of conflict situation cards

Physical Setting   Chairs arranged around a rectangular table

Content and Process
1. Create several sets of conflict situations based on the typical kinds of conflicts the participants are likely to face. For example, situations faced by women moving up the career ladder, those faced by middle managers, etc.

2. Place participants around a rectangular table, one partner facing the other. Place a stack of conflict cards in a pile between each pair.

```
2    ●    1

1    ●    2

2    ●    1

1    ●    2

2    ●    1
```

3. Discuss with the participants the objectives of this activity. Then explain the following direction:
   a. Person number 1 picks the top card and reads the roles, as described, to her or his partner across the table (person number 2).
   b. Each person takes on the role, as described, for three to five minutes.

c. When time is called, each person assesses both his or her own success and the partner's success by answering this question: Who Won? (Answers may be: I won, my partner won, we both lost, or we both won.

d. The partners then discuss their assessments and their reasons for about five minutes.

e. All participants then move one seat to the right, and should be facing a new partner. Person number one in each pair selects a new card and the process is repeated.

4. After everyone has had about four rounds, practicing with four different conflict situations, you must then decide if additional conflict cards should be used or not. Some groups will need more practice than others. A large group discussion using the following questions can provide closure to the activity:

a. Which situations were hardest to deal with? Easiest?

b. What techniques seemed to work better for you?

c. What new behaviors did you "try on"?

d. In how many situations did both you and your partner "win"?

5. The activity may be culminated by asking all participants to write out their thoughts and feelings using these sentences:

"Today I learned that I . . ."

"Tomorrow I plan to . . ."

Variations/ Comments

Suggestions for conflict situations can be drawn from the conflict style instruments found in Chapter 4, *Reacting,* and from the participants. In the latter case, ask each person to write out a real conflict they have had.

Cross-Reference Activities

1. Act it Out (this chapter)
2. Five Methods of Resolving Conflict (this chapter)

Five Methods of Resolving Conflict

Objectives

1. To apply knowledge of five methods of resolving conflict to work situations
2. To recognize one's style of resolving conflict

Group Size

Total group is divided into small groups of four to six people

Time Required

One and one-half hours.

Materials Utilized

Conflict Style Worksheet, using the one that is most appropriate (See the worksheets at the end of this activity.)

Physical Setting

Tables and chairs for each small group

Content and Process

1. Explain the purpose and objectives of activity to the participants.

2. Hand out the appropriate Conflict Style Worksheet. Explain the directions and ask that all individuals complete their own worksheet. (This requires about fifteen minutes.)

3. Divide the participants into groups of four to seven members. You may want to group them by similarities or differences to observe if the groups reach consensus in the same manner and amount of time.

4. Give the groups another copy of the appropriate Conflict Style Worksheet, and ask them to reach group consensus on each problem. Remind them of the guidelines for reaching consensus (This requires about thirty minutes.)

The "Plant/Production" version is an adaptation of "Conflict Styles: Organizational Decision Making," *1977 Annual Handbook for Group Facilitators* (LaJolla, Calif.: University Associates). The conflict worksheets for "Financial" and "Hospital" were adapted by Bill Siefert of the Mountain States Employers Council, Denver, Colorado. The conflict worksheet for "Office Personnel" was adapted by Lois Hart of Leadership Dynamics, Lyons, Colorado.

5. Give a lecturette on the five methods of resolving conflicts:
   a. Denial
   b. Suppression
   c. Power
   d. Compromise
   e. Collaboration

Use background material and the chart found in the introduction to this chapter to emphasize the concept of win/lose. Discuss situations in which each method might be used most appropriately.

6. Ask the groups to apply their knowledge of the five methods by identifying which alternative behavior is most representative of each of the five methods in each case problem.

7. Request each group to report its ranking and identify the chosen method.

8. Discuss the appropriateness of the chosen method for the described situation.

9. Relate to other examples and problems participants have experienced.

Variations/ Comments

You might assign one observer to each group to note and later report on the roles individuals displayed and how the group resolved its own conflicts.

Cross-Reference Activities

1. What Is Your Conflict Style? (Chapter 4)
2. *Managing Conflict Awareness Profile,* designed by Bob Richards

Conflict Styles
Worksheet—Plant/Production

Case One

Pete is one of your subordinates who has worked for you for two years. In the past he has been a better-than-average employee, but for the last ten days he's given just marginal performance. You know he wants to work in Maintenance. To straighten him out, you would:

_____ A) Tell him that if he wants to stay on the payroll, he'd better improve fast.

_____ B) Tell him that if he improves you'll try to get him transferred to Maintenance.

_____ C) Tell him his performance has fallen off considerably and ask if there is anything bothering him.

_____ D) Say nothing, but wait for him to improve on his own.

Case Two

You've noticed that two of your subordinates, Sally and Paul, are always arguing about the best way to do one of their assigned jobs. This has caused a slowdown in production and disrupts the work of others. To resolve the situation you would:

_____ A) Sit down with Sally and Paul and ask them to select the best ideas of both.

_____ B) Decide which one is right and tell the other to go along with the idea and quit arguing.

_____ C) Let them resolve their own problem.

_____ D) Ask each one individually what the problem is, then openly discuss their differences together.

_____ E) Point out that they are both good employees and ask for their cooperation.

Case Three

The supervisor of a department adjacent to yours, Tom Brown, permits his employees to take longer than the allotted time for coffee breaks. You insist that your employees strictly observe break times, and this has caused some resentment. At times you lend Tom an employee or two when he's in a bind. You would:

_____ A) Tell your employees that what Tom does is none of their business.

_____ B) Tell Tom you will continue helping him out if he will enforce break times.

_____ C) Talk to Tom; tell him about the problem and ask for cooperation.

_____ D) Tell your employees that the work in Tom's department probably isn't as important as theirs.

_____ E) Go to Tom's boss and ask him to make Tom adhere to break times.

Adapted from J. E. Jones and J. W. Pfeiffer, eds., *The 1977 Annual Handbook for Group Facilitators* (San Diego, Calif.: University Associates, 1977). Used with permission.

Case Four   Mary was assigned to your unit six months ago from another department where her performance had been satisfactory. You have given her two oral reprimands, one written reprimand, and a two-day suspension for unexcused absences. She called in yesterday and said she couldn't come in because of "car trouble." She has just come in to work twenty minutes late. You would:

_____ A) Say nothing now but see if she improves.
_____ B) Tell her that if she comes to work every day on time for the next sixty days you will take no action.
_____ C) Call her in and discuss the seriousness of her behavior and ask how you can help.
_____ D) Warn her that if she doesn't improve she's going to be in trouble.
_____ E) Recommend to your boss that she be terminated.

Conflict Styles
Worksheet—Office

Instructions: You are to put yourself in the place of Sally, an office manager of a large department. Read each case and then rank the five alternative courses of action, from the most desirable or appropriate way of dealing with the conflict situation to the least desirable. Rank the most desirable course of action "1," the next most desirable "2," and so on, ranking the least desirable or least appropriate action "5." Enter your rank for each item in the space next to each choice.

Case One Sally is an office manager and has noticed a pattern developing in that Sam, the mail clerk from another department, regularly stops in Sally's department to chat with one of her typists, Terry. Unfortunately, Terry's work is often late being done and other typists are beginning to resent this nonbreak-time chatter. If you were Sally, you would:

_____ A) Talk to Terry and tell her to limit her conversations during on-the-job time.

_____ B) Ask the office manager of the other department to tell Sam to stay in line.

_____ C) Approach Terry (as well as Sam, if necessary), find out what is going on, and discuss your expectations.

_____ D) Say nothing now; it would be silly to make something big out of something so insignificant.

_____ E) Try to put the rest of the office personnel at ease; it is important that they all work well together.

Case Two As office manager, Sally has encouraged her employees to make suggestions for improving office procedures. On separate occasions, two of her office personnel approached her with different suggestions for a new filing and retrieval system. Sally sees the value of both ideas, although the suggestions were very different methods, and both individuals think theirs is the best. Unfortunately, this is one more example of competition between these two people. If you were Sally, you would:

_____ A) Decide which system you will use, then announce your decision to the two employees.

_____ B) Wait and see; the best solution will become apparent.

_____ C) Tell both employees not to get uptight about their disagreement; it is not that important.

_____ D) Get the employees together and examine both of their ideas closely.

_____ E) Try one system for four or five months, and the other at a later date for an equal period of time.

Adapted by Lois Hart.

Case Three   Diane is in charge of the CRT machine, requiring accuracy and attention to detail. Mistakes are costly. Lately, Sally, the office manager, has noticed an increase in the number of mistakes. She suspects that Diane may be taking drugs on the job, or at least showing up for work under the influence of drugs. Sally feels she has some strong indications, but knows she does not have a clear-cut case. If you were Sally, you would:

_____ A) Confront Diane outright, tell her what you suspect and why and that you are concerned for her, and ask how you might help.

_____ B) Ask that the suspected offender keep her habit off the job; what she does on the job is part of your business.

_____ C) Not confront the individual right now; it might either "turn her off" or drive her underground.

_____ D) Give Diane the "facts of life"; tell her it is illegal and unsafe and that if she gets caught, you will do everything you can to see that she is fired.

_____ E) Keep a close eye on Diane to see that she is not endangering herself or others.

Case Four   As office manager, Sally periodically has lent some of her office staff to other departments who have faced urgent deadlines. These requests were small, temporary, and infrequent, causing minimal strain on her department. However, one department has recently requested an almost constant demand for two people. This means the rest of the staff must fill in for the missing people, usually by working harder and taking shorter breaks. If you were Sally, you would:

_____ A) Let it go for now; the "crisis" will probably be over soon.

_____ B) Try to smooth things over with your own staff and with the other department office manager; we all have jobs to do and cannot afford a conflict.

_____ C) Let the other department have one of the two people they requested.

_____ D) Go to the other office manager and talk about how these demands for additional personnel could best be met without placing your department in a bind.

_____ E) Ask your boss to "call off" these extra requests from the other department.

Conflict Styles
Worksheet—Health Care Institutions

Instructions: Your task is to rank the five alternative courses of action under each of the three cases below, from the most desirable or appropriate way of dealing with the conflict situation to the least desirable. Rank the most desirable course of action "1," the next most desirable "2," and so on, ranking the least desirable or least appropriate action "5." Enter your rank for each item in the space next to each choice.

Case One

You are the Head Nurse on a ward and you have recently noticed one of your nurses, Betty Brown, is spending a lot of time "socializing" with Pete Smith, a ward clerk. Pete is assigned to another ward on the same floor as yours. You think your other nurses resent the fact that Nurse Brown is not carrying her share of the work load. Your best course of action is to:

_____ A) Talk to Nurse Brown and tell her to limit her conversations during on the job time.
_____ B) Tell Pete's supervisor to keep him in line.
_____ C) Confront Nurse Brown and Pete and discuss how their conduct affects the work and ask for their cooperation.
_____ D) Say nothing now; it would be silly to make a big deal out of something so insignificant.
_____ E) Try to pacify the other nurses and impress upon them the need for teamwork.

Case Two

You are the supervisor of the Intensive Care Unit. Two of your nurses, Nancy and Mary, are engaged in a violent argument but not in front of patients. Nancy accuses Mary of returning a transfusion unit to the storeroom without cleaning it. Mary says she had to care for a patient and she thought Nancy should clean it because she didn't have anything better to do. In this case you would:

_____ A) Let them resolve their own problem.
_____ B) Suggest that they arrange a system whereby they could share the task equitably.
_____ C) Inform Mary that hospital policy requires that transfusion units be cleaned before returning to storeroom.
_____ D) Get Nancy and Mary together to discuss all aspects of the problem and solicit solutions from them.
_____ E) Tell Nancy and Mary to calm down, they are both important to the job and need to work together.

Adapted from the original by Bill Seifert, 2085 Ash St., Denver Colorado 80207. Courtesy of Mountain States Employers Council, Inc.

Case Three You are the Chief of Radiology and you suspect that one of your technicians, Al Jones, is taking nonprescribed drugs. Your suspicions are based on Al's occasional lethargy and his somewhat vague attitude when you talk with him. You should:

_____ A) Ask Al to voluntarily submit to a drug-control program and you will take no further action.

_____ B) Have a heart-to-heart talk with Al, tell him of your suspicions, and ask how you can help.

_____ C) Do nothing now, as you have no definite proof.

_____ D) Supervise Al closely to ensure he doesn't endanger himself or others.

_____ E) Tell Al he has to make a decision now: either stop taking nonprescribed drugs, or be terminated.

Case Four You are the Head Nurse on a ward. In the past, the Chief of Nursing Service has called on you to send a nurse or two down to Emergency to help out. Initially this caused no particular problem since the demands were infrequent and just for a short time. Lately, however, the demands have increased and the nurses have been gone for extended periods. As a result, the remaining nurses have had to assume a much greater work load to cover for the absent nurses, and they have complained to you about it. Your best approach would be to:

_____ A) Ask a doctor who has several patients on your ward to intercede with the Chief of Nursing Service for you.

_____ B) Accept the situation for the moment, as things will probably return to normal soon.

_____ C) Tell your nurses that you appreciate their hard work, but explain that they must keep in mind the entire hospital needs.

_____ D) Ask the Chief of Nursing Service if you can reward your nurses with extra time off for their extra effort.

_____ E) Discuss the situation with the Chief of Nursing Service, explain your problem, and suggest other alternatives.

Conflict Styles Worksheet—Financial

Instructions: Your task is to rank the five alternative courses of action under each of the three cases below, from the most desirable or appropriate way of dealing with the conflict situation to the least desirable. Rank the most desirable course of action "1," the next most desirable "2," and so on, ranking the least desirable or least appropriate action "5." Enter your rank for each item in the space next to each choice.

Case One   You are the supervisor of residential loans. Recently, you have noticed that one of the proof operators has been coming over to your department and talking to one of your title clerks (*not* on break time). The efficiency of the title clerk seems to be falling off, and there have been some errors due to this inattention. You detect some resentment among the rest of the department. To correct this you would:

_____   A) Talk to the title clerk and ask him to limit his conversations during on-the-job time.

_____   B) Ask the supervisor of the proof operator to keep his or her people in line.

_____   C) Confront your title clerk the next time you see him talking on the job, and find out what is going on.

_____   D) Say nothing now; it would be foolish to make something big out of something so insignificant.

_____   E) Try to put the rest of the department at ease; it is important that they all work well together.

Case Two   You are the Accounting Department bookkeeping manager at the main office. On separate occasions, two of your people have come to you with different suggestions for changing the accounts payable recording procedure. The suggestions are somewhat contradictory and a minor disagreement exists between the two employees in question. However, both ideas seem good, and you can find no ironclad formula on how to record accounts payable. You would:

_____   A) Decide who is right and ask the other person to go along with the decision (perhaps establish it as a written procedure).

_____   B) Wait and see; the best solution will become apparent.

_____   C) Tell both employees not to get uptight about their disagreement; it is not that important.

_____   D) Get the employees together and examine both of their ideas closely.

_____   E) Try one recording system for four or five months, and the other at a later date for an equal period of time.

Adapted from the original by Bill Seifert, 2085 Ash St., Denver, Colorado 80207. Courtesy of Mountain States Employers Council, Inc.

Case Three   You are branch manager in a bank with seven separate branch operations. From time to time in the past, the main branch has "tapped" your tellers when there have been unusually heavy days. This has put very little strain on your operation, since the demands have been small, temporary, and infrequent. Lately, however, there seems to have been an almost constant demand for two of your tellers. The rest of the staff must fill in for these missing people, usually by working harder and taking shorter breaks. In this situation, you would:

_____ A) Let it go for now; the "crisis" will probably be over soon.

_____ B) Try to smooth things over with your own staff and the main branch; everyone has a job to do and cannot afford a conflict.

_____ C) Let the main branch have one of the two tellers they requested.

_____ D) Go to the teller supervisor at the main branch and talk about how demands for additional tellers could best be met without placing any part of the operation in a bind.

_____ E) Ask your boss to "call off" the main branch requests.

The Fishbowl

Objectives
1. To learn the process of negotiation
2. To apply the process of negotiation to either intragroup or intergroup conflicts

Group Size
No more than about thirty people

Time Required
Minimum of two hours, depending on nature of conflict

Materials Utilized
Newsprint or chalkboard

Physical Setting
The room should be set up as outlined in the following diagram. Place subgroups around the outer edges of one inner circle. The inner circle should have enough chairs for one person per subgroup, one for you (the facilitator), and one extra.

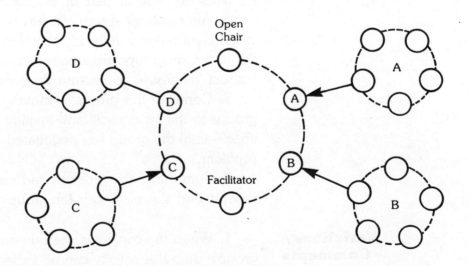

Content and Process

1. Explain the purpose of the activity and the procedures to be used to the participants.

2. You then state what you understand to be the conflict. Ask each subgroup to discuss their perception of the problem.

3. After ten to fifteen minutes, ask one representative from each subgroup to come into the inner circle where you are seated. Ask each to present her or his group's point of view. Ensure that each person is heard completely before any additional points are made. The purpose of this first step is to reach an understanding of the nature of the conflict.

4. The subgroup representatives return to their subgroups and talk about their reactions to the innergroup discussion. Tell them next to develop a proposal for discussion as to what they want to see changed.

5. The inner circle meets again to begin the negotiation process. You, as the facilitator, should then receive the proposals, perhaps using newsprint or a chalkboard to record suggestions and ideas. Now explain to the participants the additional option of the open chair. Anyone who is listening from a subgroup may come into the circle briefly to make a comment, a suggestion, or give a reaction. Such a person may only stay long enough to make a contribution—she or he does not stay as part of the inner circle.

6. After enough discussion has occurred in the center, or when clarification is needed, or when you sense that those left in the subgroups are anxious to participate again, then instruct subgroups to resume their own discussions.

7. Continue this process—moving in and out of subgroups to the inner circle and inviting others to use the open chair—until the group has negotiated a solution to the problem.

8. Summarize the problem and suggested solution, and recommend the next step for group members to take.

Variations/ Comments

1. When the conflict is not one emerging out of subgroups, then this activity can be varied so that the problem is discussed by the inner circle (A's) while an outer circle (B's) listen. After a given time, the A's stop, turn around, and the B directly behind her or him states what was heard and the subsequent reactions.

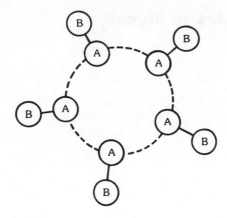

2. Another variation is to have those in the outer circle switch places with those in the inner circle.

3. Make sure that the problem being negotiated is one that is manageable. If it is too large to handle, only a part of the problem should be dealt with at a time. Also, it is important that suggested proposals and solutions are ones that are practical and within the abilities of individuals and organizations to use.

Cross-Reference Activities

1. The Counselor (this chapter)
2. Ranking and Negotiating Conflict Issues (this chapter)

Notes to Myself

Compact Problem-Solving Process

Objectives
1. To learn the five steps of the compact problem-solving process
2. To apply the problem-solving process to an unresolved conflict

Group Size
Groups of three to eight people

Time Required
Minimum of one hour, more time depending on how many people apply the process

Materials Utilized
The five-step worksheets accompanying this activity

Physical Setting
Chairs placed in circles or around tables

Content and Process

1. Present the rationale for collaborative problem solving to the participants. Its purpose is to have groups of people work together, pooling their ideas and other resources to find a solution to a conflict. This process also depends on the emotional support of all of the group members.

2. Separate the individuals into groups of three to eight people. Chairs should be arranged in a circle so everyone can easily hear and see one another. Everyone will have a chance to pose a problem, but one person has to agree to be the first. Also, two other roles are established for the first round, and later rotated. These roles include a recorder (who does any required writing) and a timer (who watches the time, indicating when the allotted time is up).

3. Each round takes thirty minutes. Each step should be completed within the time allotted, and before the next step is begun. Guide the group through each step of the first

© Lois B. Hart, "Compact Problem Solving Process," *Moving Up! Women and Leadership* (New York: AMACOM, 1980), Chapter 8.

round, calling a halt to steps and reviewing roles and procedures. After the first round, small groups can follow the steps alone, however a bell may be used to mark the end of each step.

Variations/ Comments

Groups can be formed around the same issue, or each individual can pose a different problem.

Cross-Reference Activities

1. How Many Do You See? (Chapter 5)
2. Connect the Dots (Chapter 5)
3. Act it Out (this chapter)
4. Ranking and Negotiating Conflict Issues (this chapter)
5. The Counselor (this chapter)
6. You may also teach and practice the skill of brainstorming prior to using the five-step problem-solving model.

Step One—Naming the Problem

The problem poser takes up to five minutes to describe a specific problem or incident to those in the group. These people listen carefully and avoid all talking unless clarification is needed. Such clarifying questions should assist the problem poser in the description of the problem.

Description of Incident

1. Who was involved? What did each person say and do?

2. When and where does this problem usually occur?

History of Incident

1. Is there a prior history of this incident that makes it particularly problematic?

2. What related experiences in your life preceded the incident and set the stage for it? What occurred in the other person's life prior to the incident or problem?

Consequences

1. How did you feel during and after the incident?

2. How do you think the other person(s) felt?

3. What were the sequence of events and consequences just after the incident?

Step Two—Analyzing and Goal Setting

The next five minutes are spent analyzing the causes of the problem in order to clarify what happened and why. This process encourages the problem poser to be clearer about the desired outcome.

Down to Basics

The problem poser completes each of these three sentences as many times as possible:

1. "What I really wanted in this situation was . . ."

2. "What the other person really wanted was . . ."

3. "The basic conflict is . . ."

Unique or a Pattern?

To determine if the problem is unique or part of a recurring pattern, the problem poser responds to these questions:

1. Has this incident occurred before? If so, have you and the others reacted the same way?

2. Has this problem emerged for others in your organization?

Past Attempts

It is helpful to identify practices regarding the problem.

1. What has been done in the past?

2. How did it work out?

Step Three—Searching for Solutions

The next five minutes uses the resources of all the members of the group in searching for alternative solutions to the problem described. The process used is called *brainstorming* and requires the generating of many ideas in a very short period of time. To instigate a plethora of creative ideas, this problem solving method uses the pressure of a limited amount of time and the creation of a nonjudgmental atmosphere where all ideas are counted. The goal is to create ideas in quantity, regardless of quality.

To hold a brainstorming session, one person records as quickly as possible all the ideas given by the group members. This can be done on a chalkboard, newsprint pad, or regular paper. Abbreviations may be necessary in order to keep up with the group's suggestions. All group members follow these ground rules:

1. *Quantity, not quality.* Use the time to think of as many solutions as possible. The more bizarre, the better.

2. *Piggyback.* If someone else's idea triggers a slight variation of an idea for you, call it out.

3. *No evaluation.* All ideas are accepted. No judgments of ideas are allowed at this time. Do not stop to discuss the pros and cons of any suggestion.

4. *Stop immediately.* At the end of five minutes, all brainstorming should end.

Step Four—Planning

In the fourth step of the Compact Problem-Solving Process, the problem poser reviews all the alternatives suggested in order to select those solutions having the greatest potential. Using from five to seven minutes, the problem poser evaluates each suggestion according to his or her own criteria, or the following:

1. *Impossible.* Cross out those suggestions which are unrealistic or incompatible with your values or situation.

2. *Maybe.* Put an *M* next to those you might consider.

3. *Outstanding.* Put an asterisk (*) next to those that strike you as creative, realistic, or appealing.

The problem poser and group members then discuss the most plausible solutions, refining the best ones to the point where the problem poser believes they can work. From these, the problem poser chooses at least one workable solution. This goal or plan is put into writing by the problem poser or recorder.

Step Five—Evaluation

In the last few minutes, the goal and plan are reviewed. Members determine a way in which they can find out what happened. Too often, resolutions to try something can be lost in everyday routine or in the recurrence of a person's behavioral pattern. However, if the problem poser commits himself or herself to a plan *and* combines this with support from the other members of the group, chances for success increase drastically. It is crucial, therefore, to indicate when, where, and how progress on the plan's implementation will be shared with the group members. The method chosen may be a telephone call, lunch, or note, but the method chosen is less important than making sure it occurs. The advantage of a follow-up meeting is that the group as a whole can review the progress and perhaps make new suggestions if the problem poser needs to modify the plan. This followup should take place fairly soon after the plan is developed, and it should continue until the problem poser has eliminated the problem.

Notes to Myself

8

Planning for Conflict

To successfully make changes in oneself or in the organization, we must know from where we've come and where we want to go. This chapter's activities can provide the bridge between what was experienced and what will be applied to future situations. The activities can be used both at the end of individual experiences or at the end of the workshop. They are designed to be used repeatedly, to continually summarize learnings, and to plan for the future conflicts one can expect to face.

The reflection process in the activity, I Learned . . ., summarizes and clarifies learning that occurred both in content (concepts and facts) and in self-knowledge. Based on this information, participants can set some goals. The Self-Contract activity is the most simple, personal method. The Moving Ahead activity looks at desired changes in personal, interpersonal, and organizational domains. Goal-Setting for Action extends the process, looking at barriers and resources, and assesses the chosen goal. This latter is done even more completely in the Weighing My Goals activity. Finally, a more specific plan of action is developed in Stepping Stones to Action.

If there is truly going to be *learning* from conflict, then some planning for conflict must occur.

Notes to Myself

I Learned . . .

Objective   To clarify and reinforce what was learned in previous activities

Group Size   Any

Time Required   Fifteen to thirty minutes

Materials Utilized   Paper and pencil

Physical Setting   Tables and chairs

Content and Process

1. Introduce to the participants the concept that summarizing learnings is a part of the application of learning process.

2. Review the key concepts and facts presented in the activity just completed, or the whole workshop. Ask participants to rank the concepts and facts in the order of value to them at this moment. Remind them that it might be just as important to reinforce something they already knew as to learn something brand new. For you, this ranking of concepts and facts can serve as one form of evaluation to measure the extent to which learning did occur.

3. Discuss with the group how a second form of learning is that which one learns about oneself. Upon reflection, the following incomplete sentences provide a wealth of information for participants. Ask them to complete about five:

"I learned that I . . ."

"I relearned that I . . ."

"I discovered that I . . ."

"I noticed that I . . ."

"I was surprised that I . . ."

"I'm disappointed that I . . ."

4. Ask for volunteers to share their learnings with others, either in a small group or total group. This gives them a

chance to check the range of responses, commonalities, and differences.

Variations/ Comments   1. This reflection process leads smoothly into goal setting.

2. Have participants anonymously write their learning on cards. Post these cards on a bulletin board.

Cross-Reference Activities   The other activities in this chapter

Self-Contract

Objective   To write a contract identifying one change in behavior that will either prevent or resolve conflicts in the future

Group Size   Any

Time Required   Fifteen to thirty minutes

Materials Utilized   Copies of blank contracts

Physical Setting   Tables and chairs

Content and Process

1. Introduce the objective of the activity to the participants. Discuss the value of establishing a goal for oneself.

2. After each individual has had a chance to review all possible areas of one's behavior that has not always been appropriate in the past, ask them to select one area. Next, they should complete this self-contract.

> Self-Contract
>
> I, _____ , have decided to try to achieve the goal of _____.
> The first step I will take to reach this goal will be to _____
> _____ by _____. My target date for reaching the goal is _____.
> Date _____ Signed _____
> (Witnessed by) _____

3. Have the individuals obtain the signature of a witness. Next, each person should decide who will be given a copy of the contract. This person is committed to reviewing the individual's progress in obtaining the stated goal, and can assist in resolving stumbling blocks in the way of progress. Upon completion of the contract, both persons can then celebrate with one another as the completed contract is burned.

**Variations/
Comments**

You may wish to give participants a postcard on which they write out their stated contract. Upon successful completion of the contract, they then mail the postcard to you. This serves as feedback on the success of each participant's plans of action.

Moving Ahead

Objectives

1. To identify three types of changes: personal, interpersonal and organizational
2. To identify desired changes in all three categories and possible results

Group Size

Any

Time Required

Thirty minutes to one hour

Materials Utilized

Moving Ahead worksheet (accompanying this activity)

Physical Setting

Tables and chairs

Content and Process

1. Introduce the objectives of the activity to the participants.

2. Based on the activity or workshop just experienced, ask the individuals to list one change they desire to make about themselves (personal), relationships with someone else (interpersonal), and in their organization (organizational) on the Moving Ahead worksheet. In each case, individuals should describe the current situation that exists and the desired change. For example, a person may not be pleased with his or her tendency to suppress conflicts (Current Situation) and wants to decrease the frequency of suppression by 50 percent (Desired Change). The two columns to the right help participants to clarify the results if the change is made and if it isn't. In our example, this person notes that if she or he changes behavior, some results might include less tension, the resolution of conflicts before they become enlarged, and more honest relationships. Each participant should then list in the fourth column that if the current rate of suppression is continued, some conflicts would not have to be faced so soon.

3. Have the participants share their plans either in small groups or voluntarily in the large group. This provides the opportunity for further clarification and helpful suggestions.

Cross-Reference Activity
I Learned . . . (this chapter)

Moving Ahead

Types of Changes	Current Situation	Desired Change(s)	Results if Change Occurs	Results if Change Does Not Occur
Personal				
Interpersonal				
Organizational				

Notes to Myself

Goal-Setting for Action

Objective

To ensure that a plan of action follows learning about conflict

Group Size

Any size divided into trios

Time Required

Thirty minutes to one hour

Materials Utilized

Goal Setting for Action worksheet (accompanying this activity)

Physical Setting

Groups of three chairs

Content and Process

1. Introduce to the participants the importance of applying to the future what has been learned about oneself and conflict methods.

2. Review the criteria for setting a goal as listed in the Goal Setting for Action worksheet. Give a few examples.

3. Ask each person to review what they have learned about conflict. Make a list of key ideas.

4. Next, ask participants to select one area in which they would like to change. They then complete all of the sections on the Goal Setting for Action worksheet.

5. Divide the participants into trios. Instruct all individuals to review their plans. The group members may make suggestions, ask clarifying questions, and lend support to each individual's efforts to change.

6. Share the sample plans with the total group.

Variations/ Comments

1. Develop a more specific plan with the Stepping Stones to Action worksheet (in this chapter).

2. Plan a group celebration for some future date to review progress and generally celebrate accomplishments of plans.

Cross-Reference Activity

I Learned . . . (this chapter)

Goal Setting for Action

Goal setting for _____ Date _____

Success in learning from conflicts can be enhanced by taking action. Goal setting is a means to action. Some guidelines for goal setting include the following:

1. *Conceivable.* The goal is capable of being put into words.
2. *Achievable.* The goal is realistic, given your strength, abilities, and situation.
3. *Valuable.* The goal is acceptable and desirable according to your values.
4. *Tackle-able.* You deal with only one goal at a time.
5. *Growth facilitating.* The goal does not harm you, others, or society.

_____

1. My goal will be

2. This goal will be accomplished by _____.

3. How important is it to you to reach this goal? What would happen if you reached your goal? What would happen if you didn't reach your goal?

4. What personal strengths and resources do you have that will help you reach your goal?

5. What other personal strengths or resources will be needed to reach your goal?

6. What will keep you from reaching your goal?

7. What will you do to celebrate the reaching of your goal?

Weighing My Goals

Objective To assess the appropriateness and true value of a stated goal

Group Size Any

Time Required Fifteen to thirty minutes

Materials Utilized Weighing My Goals worksheet (accompanying this activity)

Physical Setting Tables and chairs

Content and Process

1. Introduce the objective of this activity to the participants. Relate it to the previous activity that identified a goal.

2. Ask participants to list up to four goals on the Weighing My Goals worksheet and check in the appropriate column the criteria that applies.

3. Separate the group into trios or small groups. Ask individuals to share their observations, make suggestions, and ask clarifying questions of each other.

4. Participants should then develop a plan of action for the most valued goal. (See Stepping Stones to Action.)

Variations/ Comments Integrate this assessment into one of the goal setting activities.

Cross-Reference Activities
1. Self-Contract (this chapter)
2. Moving Ahead (this chapter)
3. Goal-Setting for Action (this chapter)

Weighing My Goals

My Goals	1.	2.	3.	4.
1. This goal is very important to me.				
2. I am proud that it is a goal of mine.				
3. It is realistic in that I have a good chance of achieving the goal.				
4. I have chosen this goal because I want to work toward it, not just because others want me to do it.				
5. There are risks or possible negative consequences involved in achieving this goal.				
6. I have weighed the risks involved and still think the goal is worth it.				
7. This goal is consistent with the other goals I have set for myself.				
8. I am going to make a plan of action to achieve this goal.				

Stepping Stones to Action

Objectives

1. To list steps to take in order to accomplish an identified goal
2. To identify barriers as well as helping variables in accomplishing each step

Group Size

Any number, divided in trios

Time Required

Fifteen to thirty minutes

Materials Utilized

Stepping Stones to Action worksheet (accompanying this activity)

Physical Setting

Small tables and chairs

Content and Process

1. Introduce to the participants the value of identifying specific steps to successfully reach a stated goal.

2. Have each person list her or his goal on the Stepping Stones to Action worksheet, and the target date for completion. Next, the participants should list the steps needed to accomplish this goal. To the right of each step listed, individuals then list the barriers (or difficulties) they might encounter while accomplishing that step, plus those resources available to help overcome any barriers.

3. Separate the group into trios. Instruct each person to review his or her plan to accomplish a stated goal and the steps of the plan. Ask the others in the group to review the ideas, ask clarifying questions, make suggestions, and generally lend support to the goal setter.

4. Share sample plans with the total group.

Variations/ Comments

This specific plan can be used with any of this chapter's activities that clarify a goal.

Cross-Reference Activities

1. Self-Contract (this chapter)
2. Moving Ahead (this chapter)
3. Goal-Setting for Action (this chapter)

Stepping Stones to Action

Goal I Want to Achieve:_____ By This Date:_____

Steps I Must Take	Difficulties I Might Face with Each Step	Resources and People Who Could Help Me Accomplish This Step
1.		
2.		
3.		
4.		
5.		
6.		
7.		